THE NORTH WEST
& THE LAKES

EXPLORING WOODLAND

D1369180

WOODLAND
TRUST

THE NORTH WEST
& THE LAKES

Edited by Graham Blight

FRANCES LINCOLN LIMITED
PUBLISHERS

Acknowledgements

Introduction by Archie Miles
Site entries written by Sheila Ashton
Researched by Diana Moss
Edited by Graham Blight
Maps by Linda M Dawes, Belvoir Cartographics & Design
Regional maps created using Maps in Minutes data ©MAPS IN MINUTES™/
Collins Bartholomews 2007
Site maps © Woodland Trust

Photographic acknowledgements

Archie Miles: 2, 11, 31
NTPL/Joe Cornish: 42
WTPL: 1, 8, 13, 16, 26 (Enid Pyrah), 51 (Roy Battell), 53 (Pete Holmes), 55, 57
(David Noton), 59, 60 (David Bradbury), 64, 66 (David Lund), 68 (Tessa Bunney), 79,
83, 84, 88, 91, 97 (Tim Kirwin), 101, 102, 103, 105 (Andrew Tryner), 107 (Mike
Brown), 108 (Roger Warhurst), 109, 112, 114, 117.

Frances Lincoln Ltd
4 Torriano Mews
Torriano Avenue
London NW5 2RZ
www.franceslincoln.com

The North West & The Lakes
Copyright © Frances Lincoln 2008
Text © Woodland Trust 2008
Maps © see above

First Frances Lincoln edition: 2008

A catalogue record for this book is available
from the British Library.

ISBN 978-0-7112-2672-2

Printed and bound in Singapore
The paper used in this book was sourced from
sustainable forests, managed according to FSC
(Forest Stewardship Council) guidelines.

1 2 3 4 5 6 7 8 9

Half title page Butterfly at Warton Crag

Title page Johnny Wood, Borrowdale

MAP 1
Carlisle · Newcastle Upon Tyne

Penrith

Lake District · Appleby-in-Westmorland

Ulverston · Kendal · Hawes

Barrow-in-Furness · **MAP 2** · Yorkshire Dales

Forest of Bowland

Blackpool · Bradford · Leeds
Blackburn · Burnley

Liverpool · Manchester

Sheffield

Chester · Peak District

MAP 3

Contents

How to use this guide

Covering a region that encompasses the North West including the Lake District, this book is divided into three areas represented by key maps on pages 18–19, 44–45 and 74–75. The tree symbols on these maps denote the location of each wood. In the pages following the key maps, the sites nearest one another are described together (wherever practical) to make planning a day out as rewarding as possible.

For each site entry the name of the nearest town/village is given, followed by road directions and the grid reference of the site entrance. The area of the site (in hectares followed by acres) is given together with the official status of the site where appropriate and the owner, body or organisation responsible for maintaining the site. Symbols are used to denote information about the site and its facilities as explained in the next column.

Type of wood

Mainly broadleaved woodland

Mainly coniferous woodland

Mixed woodland

Car park

Parking on site

Parking nearby

Parking difficult to find

Official status

Area of Outstanding Natural Beauty AONB

Site of Special Scientific Interest SSSI

Site facilities

Sign at entry

Information board

One or more paths suitable for wheelchair users

Dogs allowed under supervision

Waymarked trail

Toilet

Picnic area

Entrance/car park charge

Refreshments on site

The North West & The Lakes

Raveden Wood

Cast a glance at the maps of the North West region covered within this guide and the first impression is of a land of stark contrasts. To the south any woodland sites appear to vie for space with the intensive network of motorways, roads and merging settlements of the Manchester and Liverpool conurbations, whilst sixty miles to the north that ever popular tourism honey pot, The Lake District, its dramatic vistas the inspiration for generations of poets and artists, has room for great tracts of woodland, some well frequented and others more remote and less familiar.

It is widely appreciated today that trees, parks and woodland are the green lungs of the urban environment. We all need green oases to refresh the body and soul, and fortunately it would seem that our forebears felt much the same, particularly those with the wherewithal to make a difference.

Many of the south Lancashire woodlands featured within were either created or bolstered by the endeavours of wealthy local landowners with a desire to acquire their very own designer tracts of countryside; often to provide cover for their game or to supply the timber and fuel needs of their estates and businesses. However, with the ever-increasing demand for available land throughout the last 200 years it seems a miracle that there is any woodland left at all, but the Victorians were well aware that sustainability was the watchword for woodland management. As with so many parts of Britain in close proximity to industry a strict coppice regime was the only way to ensure that the wood, charcoal and tan bark needed to keep mill, foundry and factory in full spate was readily available.

Extensively planted or managed woodlands once linked to estates survive in several different forms, depending upon the predilections of their owners, and may often still contain introduced or exotic species. One of the biggest mistakes these landowners did make though was their fascination with the newly arrived rhododendron. At first it was a showy and successful shrub on the acidic soils, but currently viewed with some dismay as an ever-spreading, all-suppressing weed.

One of the most spectacular examples of these large estate schemes is Lever Park, set on the slopes of Rivington Pike, once the home of the great industrial philanthropist Lord Leverhulme. Here, a landscape comprised of broadleaf woodland, avenues, parkland and gardens has been carved from the rugged hillside. Daisy Nook (what a sweet name – surely fairies must live here) was part of the estate of the now ruined Riversvale Hall and here it is still possible to trace remnants of an old arboretum amongst the naturally regenerating woodland. Raveden, near Bolton, is also a woodland once managed as an extension to the pleasure grounds of Smithills Hall; whilst Towneley Woods, near Burnley, reveals the indulgences of the owners of Towneley Hall with once grand re-landscaping schemes of the 19th century complete with a splendid array of follies and grottoes. As a modern extension to this theme there is now a new generation of woodland sculptures appearing here and there along the walks.

Although the endeavours of the great and the good made a valuable contribution to Lancashire's tree cover in the past, today it needs the concerted efforts of government policy and grass roots enthusiasm to make radical woodland expansion possible. Over the last 15 years there have been 12 Community Forests slowly evolving throughout England, two of these being The Red Rose Forest, in and around Greater Manchester, and The Mersey Forest (the largest), covering some 110,000 hectares (270,000 acres) of Merseyside and north Cheshire. A partnership between the Countryside Agency, the Forestry Commission, local authorities and many other local and national partners has provided a programme of woodland regeneration in urban areas, and with the involvement of people in the respective communities, a greener and more pleasant land for many city dwellers looks a distinct reality in the future.

As a county Lancashire is fairly sparsely wooded, and it seems likely that this has been the case for hundreds of years. Industry and agriculture pushed back the woodland cover to the most inaccessible areas on the poorest land, such as the steep acidic valley sides known locally as cloughs. Here it was difficult to actively manage the woodland, which was virtually impregnable to marauding flocks of sheep. Tree cover here is often oak, with birch in the upper reaches and sycamore, ash and wych elm prevailing along the valley bottoms. Sycamore, much pilloried in other parts of Britain, is very successful and, as well as providing excellent timber, it manifests as a distinctive shelter tree in some of the more exposed locations. Traditionally the wood was prized by the bobbin makers who crafted millions of bobbins for the cotton and wool industries.

Before heading north it's well worth a coastal detour to take in a remarkable wood at Formby. This salt-laden seaside wood predominantly of Scots pine (but also including some Maritime and Corsican pine) was planted in 1900 with the intention of stabilising

Bowder Stone

the sand dunes and, eventually, of building a promenade. That never happened, but what did happen, and largely because of the island habitat created by the developed hinterland, was the ongoing survival of a colony of red squirrels. There may be no better place to observe these delightful little characters, and what's more they are bold enough to be fed by visitors.

The middle of Lancashire may appear somewhat misleading in its appellation as the Forest of Bowland, for it is not, as some would assume, a forest of dense tree cover, but now merely an administrative region containing scattered small woodlands. The word 'forest' has become inextricably linked in the minds of most people to regions dominated by trees and woodland, yet its true meaning harks back to the Norman Conquest, when William I established the first royal forests. These were exclusive preserves held by the crown principally for the purpose of hunting, although eventually economic reasons also prevailed. By the thirteenth century a quarter of the country was designated as royal forest, and it just so happened that the majority of these were in the wilder and more wooded parts. Travel to Scotland and there are forests where you may ramble for days with barely a sight of a single tree!

However, on the northern tip of Lancashire, above Carnforth, lie the remarkable woodlands of Silverdale and Arnside, where carboniferous limestone dictates a rich diversity of vegetation. Gait Barrows (a National Nature Reserve) is one of the finest examples of limestone pavement in Britain with its associated woodland of stunted yew, ash, rowan, hazel and birch struggling improbably from the depths of the rocky grikes. Here and there a Scots pine, a juniper, a buckthorn or the locally specific Sorbus lancastriensis, one of the country's rarest whitebeams. Many of these trees, although relatively small, are probably extremely old; the arduous conditions creating natural semi-bonsai forms. The woods around the pavement areas contain the same mix of trees, but with rather more normal size and appearance. An astounding number of more than 1,600 types of fungi and 800 species of moth have been identified here, not to mention all the plants and butterflies too! It's one of those places you just have to revisit time and again. A short step away lies Eaves Wood. Yet again bands of limestone span the woodland floor, but here, unlike at Gait Barrows, a little more shelter from the elements has allowed loam to collect amongst the rocky crevices, giving rise to some splendid yews and, in the site's lower hollows, truly beautiful old small-leaved lime coppice stools. These mossy old limes are almost certainly many hundreds of years old and occur very close to the tree's northern range limit. Due to colder climatic conditions this species no longer sets viable seed and so they represent the last of their line in northern Britain, only proliferating through coppicing or natural layering. A chock-a-block car park here reflects the wood's popularity, offering such features as a mature planted circle of tall beeches (with the usual adornments made by trysting lovers) and a tower folly called the Pepper Pot, with excellent views of Morecambe Bay.

Near the village of Arnside lies a 150-metre (500 foot) limestone hill known as Arnside Knott, again with fine views across the Bay to the distant Lake District. Named because of its now defunct knotted

Bickerton Hills

larch trees, conjoined in the 19th century as a love token (old postcards illustrating these may still be found), the Knott's close proximity to habitation rather creates the impression of a public park. Tree cover varies from dense oak with hazel, rowan, holly and some splendid yews around the slopes to the sparser vegetation of the heathland on the hill top and a number of craggy old pines.

Further north, with a swing westward into the southern Lake District of Cumbria and one is revelling in the region known as The Furness. This has always been a well-wooded part of the country and certainly this was ensured up until the early 20th century by the attentive management of local industries who depended upon both the coppice wood for charcoal used in iron smelting, and tan bark for the leather industry. Latterly much of the broadleaf cover gave way to the Forestry Commission's conifer plantations, but in most recent times the balance is once again tipping back in favour of more broadleaf woodland. Typically most of Cumbria's ancient woodland is comprised of birch and sessile oak, but in the more verdant valley bottoms and hollows ash, wych elm and hazel are evident, and where limestone outcrops appear yews, often of great proportions or with gnarled and sprawling forms, imbue their woods with a sense of mystery and wonder.

Not all of Cumbria is as well endowed with woodland as The Furness for the traditional counterbalance to successful tree growth has historically been the presence of sheep. Coppice woodland was jealously guarded by those whose livelihoods depended upon it, and that wasn't just in relation to iron and leather. Coppice wood was crucial for pit props, furniture makers, coopers, cloggers, bobbin turners and basket makers; and larger timbers were always required for building houses and ships. Records show, for example, that oak timbers from Sea Wood, at Bardsea, were floated from the wood's edge at high tide and towed round to the shipyards of nearby Ulverston. These woods still tumble down to the shoreline coping happily with the salt laden air, finishing a mere metre or two above the high-tide mark. The critical interdependence of all these woodland-based crafts and industries has now largely disappeared into the pages of history books, but a recent upsurge in interest from a dedicated band of contemporary craftsmen is seeing the resurrection of many virtually forgotten skills. This in turn puts a measure of vibrancy back into many of the long-neglected coppice woods. Working woodland is healthy woodland!

The Forestry Commission has, since its inception, had a considerable presence in the Lake District. Largely as a result of a 1936 agreement between the Commission and the Council for the Preservation of Rural England, plantations of spruce, larch and Douglas fir have been restricted to the outlying areas of the region, allowing the survival of the ancient woodlands in most of the central Lake District. One extensive system which illustrates this rather well, although some limited planting has occurred in the more accessible tracts, is in the Borrowdale Woods. A day or two spent exploring these remarkable woodlands provides a fascinating overview.

Travelling southward from Keswick, Great Wood is the first encounter, with its striking zonal formation. On the shores of adjacent Derwent Water, water-loving trees such as alder and willow predominate. A little way inland and towering stands of larch guard the lower fellsides, but as gentle slopes become craggy mountains the natural woodland of oak, ash, wych elm, birch, rowan, holly and hazel takes over, and in the upper reaches Scots pine also puts in an appearance. It is very quickly apparent that this wood, like the other Borrowdale Woods, is richly endowed with wonderful colonies of mosses, lichens and liverworts, typically associated with Britain's Atlantic coast and its plentiful rainfall and pure air. Identifying some of the rarities in this field (which do occur here) will be lost on all but the experts, and yet close inspection of these tiny plants reveals an exquisite array of colour and form.

Along the valley, coaches and cars pull over so that visitors can take a brisk walk through Ashness Wood to visit the Bowder Stone, a mammoth glacial boulder carelessly left here by the glacier which shaped Borrowdale many millions of years ago. After marvelling at the size of this celebrity rock and taking a few photographs of it, on it and with it, most people file back to their cars, but Ashness Wood deserves further investigation, for it's a wonderful rocky undulating wood full of variety.

With Derwent Water behind, the tiny settlement of Seatoller is reached and hard by lies Johnny's Wood. This is principally a woodland of oak coppice, most of which has now grown into tall spindly trees due to their close proximity. In the past, grazing restricted the growth of understorey trees and shrubs, yet now the woodland floor is a green boulder-strewn carpet with a wealth of mosses and lichens.

Go that extra mile, to the end of Borrowdale, and close to the tiny settlement of Seathwaite seek out the Fraternal Four. These four impressive and ancient yew trees are found on the lower slopes of the western side of the valley, the largest having been nominated as one of Britain's Fifty Greatest Trees. However, it is recommended that you take your raincoat with you, since Seathwaite is officially the wettest inhabited place in England – receiving around 3,350mm (140 inches) of rain each year. Unbelievably, a September visit in 2002 found the river Derwent here as dry as a bone!

It is the water that shapes so many of the Lakeland woodlands, whether it be serene lakes, tumbling streams disgorging from

Helsby Hill

mountainsides or babbling rivers meandering through broad valleys. To the west lies Eskdale, as good a place as any to enjoy water and woodland at one. The river Mite threads its way along the lower reaches of Miterdale Forest; birch, wild cherry and hazel sprouting from the waterlogged banks, whilst on higher ground some fine stands of beech are found. Admittedly there is also a lot of forestry activity going on, removing much of the softwood, but compartments of broadleaves remain and it is to be hoped that future regeneration and planting will be of this type. A good network of forest tracks makes this an ideal place for mountain biking or orienteering. An eerie experience here is to be alone in the wood and hear the distant mournful whistle of a steam train chugging along the nearby Ravenglass and Eskdale Railway.

For one of the most dramatic wet woodland experiences try the winding path up through Stanley Ghyll. Hugging the course of the stream from its relatively sedate lower reaches, the path threads amongst larches and gigantic Douglas firs and soon climbs steeply through the narrowing gorge, criss-crossing the torrent via a series of bridges. Ever upward and the gorge becomes narrower and deeper, the water more thunderous, the trees and ferns more tenuously anchored to the slippery sheer granite. It's hugely exhilarating to be perfectly safe (but watch your step on some of the wet paths) yet so close to the roar of danger.

Frankly, there's never a dull moment in the Lakeland woods, which may come as a surprise to many, since the star turns of the region have traditionally been the mountains and lakes. With the fascinating vegetation, the dramatic terrain, the silvan vistas, and all the historic evidence of centuries of woodmanship seen in ancient coppice stools, old charcoal hearths and ancient trackways, there's plenty to enjoy.

Traversing the Lakeland uplands watch out for juniper – a strange little tree of the limestone which is our only native cypress. Easily mistaken for gorse bushes from a distance, juniper adopts a bizarre range of forms. Perfect, proper, tall and pointed specimens, akin to fine Italian cypresses, appear side by side with scruffy, weather-beaten, almost zoomorphic forms. Weather conditions such as persistent winds and heavy snows are the most likely explanation.

Weather has shaped many different exposed trees and it is often astounding to see how tenacious some Lakeland trees can be. One of the most dramatically successful species is the rowan, which appears to have the ability to thrive in the most exposed, barren and seemingly impossible locations. Trees often grow from tiny rock crevices in huge boulders or rock faces and there are many occurrences of quite large rowans growing within the forks of host trees of other species. How the root systems make it to terra firma or draw enough sustenance is a miracle.

Weird woodland experience of the year: the author, walking down Haverthwaite Heights, soaking up the early morning autumn sunshine, was suddenly stopped in his tracks as a peacock strutted haughtily across the path in front. You just never know for sure what's around the next woodland corner.

ARCHIE MILES

MAP 1

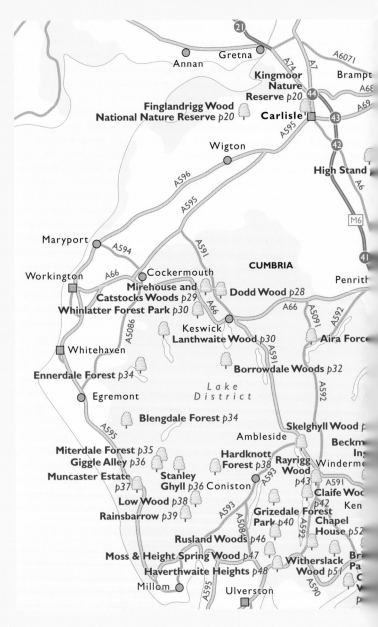

Annan
Gretna
21
A74
A7
A6071
Bramp

Kingmoor Nature Reserve *p20*
44
A68

Finlandrigg Wood National Nature Reserve *p20*
Carlisle
A69
43

A595
42

Wigton
A6

High Stand

A596

A595
M6

Maryport
A594
A591
41

Workington
A66
Cockermouth
CUMBRIA

Mirehouse and Catstocks Woods *p29*
Dodd Wood *p28*
Penrith

Whinlatter Forest Park *p30*
A66
A66
A5091
A592

A5086
Keswick

Whitehaven
Lanthwaite Wood *p30*
Aira Force

Ennerdale Forest *p34*
Borrowdale Woods *p32*

Egremont
Lake District
A592

Blengdale Forest *p34*
Skelghyll Wood *p*
Beckm

A595
Ambleside
In

Miterdale Forest *p35*
Hardknott Forest *p38*
Rayrigg Wood
Winderme

Giggle Alley *p36*
A591

Muncaster Estate *p37*
Stanley Ghyll *p36*
Coniston
A593
p43
Claife Woo
p42
Ken

Low Wood *p38*
A593
Grizedale Forest Park *p40*
Chapel House *p52*

Rainsbarrow *p39*
A508
A592

Rusland Woods *p46*
Br

Moss & Height Spring Wood *p47*
Witherslack Wood *p51*
Pa

Haverthwaite Heights *p48*
Millom
A595
Ulverston
A590

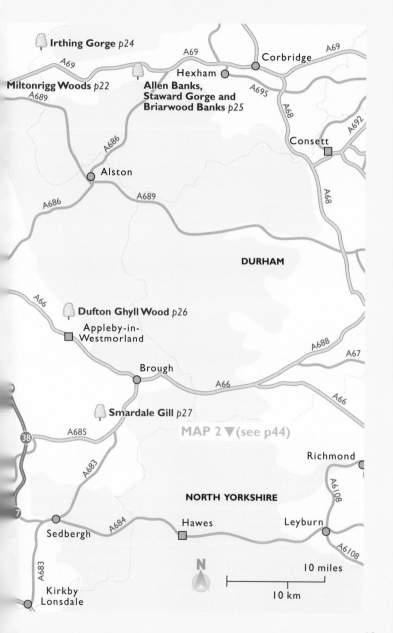

Irthing Gorge *p24*

A69

Corbridge

A69

Miltonrigg Woods *p22*

Hexham

Allen Banks,
Staward Gorge and
Briarwood Banks *p25*

A695

A68

A692

A689

A686

Consett

A68

Alston

A689

A686

A689

DURHAM

A66

Dufton Ghyll Wood *p26*

Appleby-in-
Westmorland

A688

A67

Brough

A66

A66

Smardale Gill *p27*

MAP 2 ▼(see p44)

38

A685

Richmond

A683

NORTH YORKSHIRE

A6108

Sedbergh

A684

Hawes

Leyburn

7

A6108

A683

Kirkby
Lonsdale

N

10 miles

10 km

19

MAP 1

Finglandrigg Wood National Nature Reserve
Carlisle

The site is well signed from the Haverlands Green lay-by on B5307 Carlisle to Kirkbride road. (NY282572)
97ha (240acres) SSSI
English Nature

Wonderful for walks, Finglandrigg National Nature Reserve is an island of rich habitats in an otherwise featureless landscape.

One of the largest areas of semi-natural woodland on the Solway Plain, the reserve is made up of a mosaic of habitats that support a range of wildlife, including numerous bird species and red squirrels that thrive among the Scots pine.

Formerly agricultural land and peat bog, the reserve is a mixture of naturally regenerated birch, rowan, willow, oak and beech, broken up with sections of pine which have developed from original planting in the early 19th century to become natural-looking stands on the woodland edges.

Visitors can spend many hours exploring the woodland and adjoining lowland heath of Little Bampton Common via an excellent network of footpaths and enjoy one of many lovely picnic spots.

Most walks are on level ground, though off the surfaced tracks the going can get muddy. Exploration is helped by a good supply of information panels.

Kingmoor Nature Reserve
Carlisle

Go north on A7 over River Eden, turn left at second traffic lights into Etterby Road and follow road (becomes Kingmoor Road) to urban fringe. The reserve is opposite a large warehouse. (NY388578)

43ha (106acres)
Carlisle City Council

This light and airy local woodland of oak and birch, young beech and sycamore has excellent access and is packed with history.

This was once common land, known as Royal Kings Moor, where local people had grazing and peat cutting rights until it was enclosed in the 18th century and part of the site was even used as a racecourse until 1850.

Kingmoor has been a reserve since 1913, making it one of the oldest nature reserves in Britain. There are a variety of habitats to enjoy here including ponds, grasslands and wetlands.

A network of well-surfaced paths and three waymarked trails allow gentle walking and good access for buggies and wheelchair users. Seats are thoughtfully provided throughout the reserve.

High Stand
Armathwaite/Wetheral

Follow signs for Armathwaite off A6. Take first left in village and continue for 2.5km (1.5 miles). At sign to FE car park turn right. Car park is 1.6km (1 mile) on the left. (NY498495)
250ha (618acres)
Forestry Commission

There are majestic stands of Scots pine in this predominantly coniferous forest, which provide an ideal habitat for the red squirrel. Evidence of stripped cones on the woodland floor show they're not far away.

Beneath the pines, broadleaved trees such as beech, oak, rowan, birch and holly are making a comeback, creating a more natural looking woodland. The ground flora features acidic-loving bracken and bilberry – seek out the berries in autumn, growing alongside bramble, sorrel and ferns.

There is a network of generally easy footpaths to help you explore this large wood. A few enjoyable hours could be spent here, including perhaps a summer picnic on grassy areas just a minute or two from the car park. The car park features a number of wild cherry trees that have a good crop in late summer.

There are occasional views across the Eden Valley, which also offers good walking.

MAP 1

Miltonrigg Woods
Brampton
A69 from Brampton, turn right on minor road heading south, car park
30m on right. (NY559612)
63ha (157acres)
The Woodland Trust

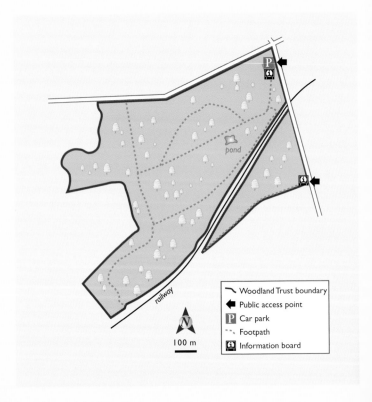

Just a few miles south of historic Hadrian's Wall is a landmark of Nature's making – Miltonrigg Wood, an outstanding feature of the Cumbrian landscape.

A network of paths lead you through this peaceful ancient woodland. The wood is accessible for all abilities and includes a surfaced route, which is suitable for wheelchair users and visitors with buggies.

The wood is dominated by wonderful beech and oak trees, many over 100 years old. Oak timber harvested from this site is reputed to have been used for the rebuilding of sections of York Minster roof. Some areas were planted with conifers in the post-war years and rhododendron dominated the wood in the past. The Woodland Trust is undertaking a careful programme of work to restore the woodland's ancient communities.

Elsewhere, areas have been left undisturbed allowing the dead and dying trees to create habitats for small insects and mammals. Visitors may be lucky enough to spot the occasional roe deer.

More than 200 species of flowering plant grow here – including seven species of sedge and five of rush as well as wood sorrel, wood anemone, bluebell and early purple orchid along the path edges. Marsh cinquefoil, which takes its name from the five sharp purple petals of its bloom can also be spotted by the keen eye in wetter sections of the wood.

Miltonrigg is alive with birds including kestrel, sparrowhawk, tawny owl, great spotted woodpecker, redstart and coal tit among the more common woodland birds. Summer visitors might be lucky enough to witness the evening display flight of a woodcock.

A pond at the heart of the wood provides a habitat for dragonflies, toads and newts.

MAP 1

Irthing Gorge
Gilsland

Either park in the village of Gilsland and follow the public footpath which passes Wardrew House or turn off B6318 in Gilsland toward Gilsland Spa. If you can find a space to park near the hotel you can walk into the wood from here. (NY634685)
34ha (84acres) SSSI
The Woodland Trust

History, romance, spectacular scenery, watersports and an abundance of wildlife – Irthing Gorge has it all.

This ancient woodland, a Site of Special Scientific Interest in the Northumberland National Park, forms part of a mosaic of wildlife habitats. It lines the steep sides of a deep gorge chiselled by the fast-flowing River Irthing. At its head is a waterfall known as Crammel Linn. Now the Woodland Trust is planting native trees on adjoining grassland to buffer and extend the ancient woodland.

Red squirrels and badgers inhabit the gorge, alongside a varied bird population and a rich mix of woodland plants. Yew grows on the cliff edges while ash dominates the lower slopes and birch is to be found on higher ground.

The gorge lies four miles north of Gilsland, one of 19th-century Britain's most fashionable spa resorts. Still popular, its scenery is as romantic as ever.

Allen Banks, Staward Gorge & Briarwood Banks
Haydon Bridge

6.5km (4 miles) west of Haydon Bridge on the A69, turn south onto minor road signed Allen Banks. Having crossed river, take left fork and follow road to National Trust Allen Banks car park. To reach Briarwood Banks either walk along river from Allen Banks car park or follow signs to Plankey Mill and park at farm (NY791620). Cross river bridge to reserve. Staward Gorge can be accessed from either car park. (NY797640/NY791620)
200ha (494acres) SSSI
The National Trust/ Northumberland Wildlife Trust

Popular with walkers, these woods flank the deep-sided slopes along the River Allen and its tributary valleys.

Dormice, red squirrel, otter, roe deer, badger, mink and stoat are among the animals at home here, together with more than 60 species of bird.

A network of occasionally steep and muddy paths leads through the woodland and beside the river. Try the 4km (2.5mile) route from Allen Banks car park through Victorian ornamental woodland to Plankey Mill – this encompasses the entire site. More adventurous visitors can continue to Staward Gorge, a more rugged area to the south, to look for the ruins of a medieval peel tower and gatehouse.

Woodlands here are largely ancient with oak and wych elm growing above a rich ground flora including moschatel, while 18th-century beech and conifers prevail elsewhere. One of the joys of this site is at Allen Banks, encountering the meadow where wild pansies grow adjacent to a stand of conifers.

MAP 1

Dufton Ghyll Wood
Dufton

On the steep sides of Dufton Gill, just south of the village of Dufton, near Appleby. (NY685251)
10ha (26acres) AONB, SSSI
The Woodland Trust

Dufton Ghyll Wood is one of the few remaining outposts in the North West for the native red squirrel.

Lining the steep, sheltered sides of a valley on the western edge of the Pennines, the site is

Dufton Ghyll Wood

as exciting for its geology as its trees. It is designated regionally important for St Bee's sandstone (a deposit laid down by a river flowing through a vast desert plain) – hailed as 'the best exposure in the Eden Valley'.

By the time the Woodland Trust took on the site in 1980, most of the trees had been felled but a replanting programme has seen the surviving mature beech, oak, sycamore, sweet chestnut and elm complemented by young, native broadleaves.

In spring the ground is covered with the brightly coloured blooms of winter aconites, daffodils, wood anemones, bluebells, pignut and angelica – with mosses, ferns and liverworts in damper areas.

Smardale Gill
Kirkby Stephen

Turn off A685 (signposted Waitby and Smardale) approx. 800m (0.5 mile) south of Kirkby Stephen. Follow signs to Smardale taking first turning left and then second turning left to car park. (NY738083) 20ha (49acres) SSSI

Cumbria Wildlife Trust

Dramatic Smardale Gill is full of interest, where part of the old Stainmore railway line leads visitors through a peaceful landscape with only the river, birds and sheep supplying background noises.

Access is via a 'green tunnel' created by the trees and scrub that now enclose this stretch of the old railway line.

The walk follows the steep, densely wooded and flora-rich valley of Scandal Beck while, higher up, the Smardale viaduct adds drama, and panoramic views are provided as trees give way to pasture.

The woodland is rich in wildlife – including red squirrel and roe deer – and a wonderful array of flora such as orchids and harebell. St John's wort grows alongside the railway cutting, attracting the rare Scotch Argus butterfly.

Within the reserve, the wood opens out, providing bird's eye views across the valley to the hills beyond. Permissive paths allow circular walks incorporating more open grassland areas.

MAP 1

Aira Force
Glenridding / Pooley Bridge

Well signposted from the A592
along the west shore of Ullswater.
(NY401200)
100ha (247acres)
The National Trust

Woodland tends to take a back
seat to waterfalls at Aira Force.
But the woods, lovely in their
own right, are well worth
exploring on a visit to this
spectacular landscape.

The area, already a popular
tourist spot in the late 18th
century, became a celebrated
destination during the 19th
century when the Howard
family created an arboretum on
the hillside below.

The arboretum is dominated
by conifers, including some
splendid Douglas fir, cedars and
a spectacular giant Sitka spruce.

Take advantage of the well-
surfaced paths to climb up the
hillside towards High Force.
Mosses, lichens and ferns thrive
in the moist air alongside the
churning waters and often
festoon oaks growing alongside
hazel and birch trees.

There is plenty to explore
beyond the falls and woods,
not least the alder woods of
Gowbarrow where you might
spot red squirrels among the
trees and dippers along the
becks where primroses grow.

Dodd Wood
Bassenthwaite / Keswick

Signposted from the A591 from
Keswick at Mirehouse.
(NY245273)
260ha (643acres) SSSI
Forestry Commission

Gentle strolls, strenuous walks,
stunning lakeland and mountain
views – all can be enjoyed in a
visit to Dodd Wood.

Planted with conifers in the
1920s, the mixed plantations
have been softened through
more recent, sensitive
management, which is
designed to complement the
Cumbrian landscape.

A network of paths and
rides through the plantation
provide easy, sheltered walking
by the towering firs of Skill
Beck and Longside Wood. The
paths are well made and
generally easy underfoot,

taking in broadleaf glades and cool conifer avenues.

The climb up to the top of the fell is more strenuous but from here you can enjoy wonderful views of Derwent Water and the hills of Dumfries and Galloway.

Plan a visit before the end of summer and you may be rewarded with the sight of an Osprey. If the weather is good, the birds can be observed from a special viewpoint across the lake.

Mirehouse & Catstocks Woods
Bassenthwaite / Keswick

Mirehouse is off the A59. Follow signs to Mirehouse from A66 at Keswick. (NY236282)

13ha (32acres) SSSI

Mr J Fryer-Spedding

A combined visit to house, garden and woodland offers a rewarding trip for the whole family. There is plenty to interest younger members of the family with free children's nature notes and, within the gardens, a woodland adventure playground.

The route through the grounds features ornamental woodland alongside a beck with lovely old trees towards Catstocks Wood and a lake edged with birch and hazel, finally leading to a small plantation with impressively large, old larch trees.

The walks are mostly easy, with a well-made path suitable for buggies and wheelchairs which meanders through the wood, eventually emerging at a lake.

MAP 1

Whinlatter Forest Park
Braithwaite / Keswick

Follow signs from A66 Keswick to
Cockermouth Road. (NY210250)
1200ha (2966acres)
Forestry Commission

This was the Forestry
Commission's first Lake
District planting in 1919.

Sitka spruce plantations
tower up to 1,700 feet above
you with larch, Douglas fir,
hemlock and red cedar on the
lower levels and broadleaves
bordering roads and rides.

Today it is well used for
walks, cycling, orienteering
and timber production.

A series of well waymarked
routes provide opportunities
to escape the crowds and
explore areas of broadleaves,
conifer stands and open
glades. Many lead to the
summits of surrounding fells,
others provide sheltered
walking and the chance to
observe wildlife.

During the breeding season
you can enjoy live CCTV
pictures of ospreys from the
Whinlatter Visitor Centre.

Lanthwaite Wood
Lorton, south of Cockermouth

Take the B5289 from
Cockermouth through Lorton
towards Loweswater. Car park on
left just past Scale Hill.
(NY150216)
28ha (69acres)
The National Trust

At the northern end of
Crummock Water and
extending along the eastern
shore for a short distance, this
mixed woodland of oak, birch,

beech, larch, Scots pine and
spruce is a pleasant spot.

A wide ride leads you to the
lakeside where benches
provide a resting place
overlooking the water and a
lovely view of the Buttermere
Fells. A short circular walk can
also be enjoyed by following a
narrower path along the
riverside back to the car park.

Other walks take you further
into the wood, to the boat
house and beyond. This is fairly
easy walking with no steep
climbs but the riverside walk
can be muddy in places.

An intriguing ash/rowan tree in Borrowdale (see next page)

MAP 1

Borrowdale Woods
Keswick

From A527 take B5289 to Borrowdale. Ashness Wood is the largest area of wood in the middle section of the valley. There are 3 car parks that can be used to visit different parts of the wood. (NY254168)
650ha (1607acres) SSSI
The National Trust

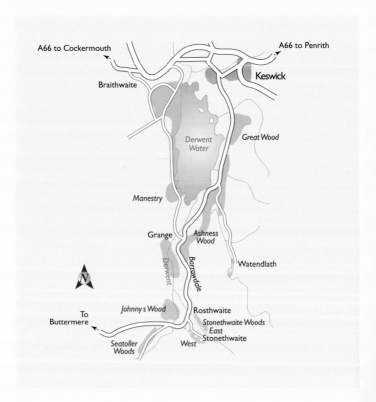

A66 to Cockermouth

A66 to Penrith

Braithwaite

Keswick

Derwent Water

Great Wood

Manestry

Grange

Ashness Wood

Watendlath

Derwent

Borrowdale

N

To Buttermere

Johnnys Wood

Rosthwaite

Stonethwaite Woods
East Stonethwaite

Seatoller Woods

West

The wet Cumbrian climate has shaped a unique and spectacular woodland experience. Borrowdale Woods, nuzzling Derwent Water and stretching from Keswick to Seathwaite, are the region's own rainforests.

Extending over 650 hectares, this complex of upland oakwood contains lush lichen and moss-covered trees growing dramatically on steep, boulder-strewn slopes.

The woods were intensively managed for centuries to support local industry but later neglected. Sheep grazing prevented regrowth and this was followed by limited conifer planting. Work is ongoing to revitalise the woods by encouraging natural regeneration.

Each of the woods has its own character and atmosphere, thanks to different management methods employed in the past, with flora and fauna changing along with the gradient.

The area known as Lodore-Troutdale or Ashness Wood contains ancient woodland and is important for birds and insects, particularly the hairy wood ant. Red deer can often be seen. An array of short walks is possible, using a variety of paths and tracks, including a half-mile walk, suitable for wheelchairs and buggies, to the Bowder Stone – a huge, impressive glacial boulder.

Great Wood, a mixture of conifers and ancient semi-natural woodland, is renowned for the tree-dwelling lichens that thrive in its heart. Conditions vary from the lake shore where willow and alder dominate to drier fellside areas with oak and ash. Many routes lead through the wood including a path along to Walla Crag with its wonderful views of Borrowdale and Derwent Water.

Beautiful to walk through, Johnny's Wood is littered with moss-covered boulders overhung by branches of mature oak and provides good views across the valley. It is these sumptuous mosses, lichens, liverworts and ferns that give the wood its unique and rare character.

Manesty Wood, on the shores of Derwent Water, is a mixed broadleaf and conifer woodland whose well-surfaced paths allow good access to the shore for buggies and wheelchairs.

MAP 1

Ennerdale Forest
Ennerdale Bridge
Follow road out of Ennerdale
Bridge toward lake for 6.5km
(4 miles) to Bowness Knot.
(NY110153)
2674ha (6609acres) SSSI
Forestry Commission

Providing a striking backdrop
to stunning Cumbrian lakeland
scenery, Ennerdale Forest has
much to offer those willing to
leave the forest road and
explore.

One of the region's largest
conifer forests, Ennerdale was
planted in the 1920s and is
dominated by larch, Scots pine
and sitka. But this huge site is
much more attractive than it
first seems, as a walk within the
woodland reveals.

Since the 1970s, work has
been carried out to mould a
forest more in tune with the
Cumbrian landscape and there
are areas of broadleaved
woodland – by the lake, beside
becks and along forest rides –
that add variety to the scene.

These can be discovered by
following the waymarked trails
– strong boots recommended –
that provide wonderful views.
One of these – the Smithy
Beck Trail – is a delightful
short walk past the beck,
which can easily be extended
to take in broadleaf areas.

Blengdale Forest
Gosforth
Take Wasdale Road from Gosforth
and turn left by Walkmill Garden
Centre before road bends right to
cross bridge. Continue along this
road until you reach the parking
area on the right. (NY090070)
424ha (1043acres)
Forestry Commission

This may be a commercial
plantation, but a walk through
the valley of the River Bleng
can be rewarding, with
magnificent tree specimens
towering above you.

Here you can see how rich
and varied conifer woodland
can become if thinned and
allowed to develop beyond the
age at which it would
normally be felled.

The trees climb the steep
valley sides up from the river,

the sound of running water filling the air. The river is a wonderful focal point for the valley walk and particularly dramatic on wet days. However, water can flow onto the path after heavy rainfall so

wellies or walking boots are strongly recommended.

According to the map, a circular walk is possible but involves a difficult scramble so it is probably better to return along the same route.

Miterdale Forest
Eskdale Green

From A595 take minor road to Eskdale. Approx. 800m (0.5 mile) past Bower House Inn take minor road on left – this leads past the school and into Miterdale. (NY147012)
321ha (793acres)
Forestry Commission

Standing along the banks of the River Mite is Miterdale Forest, a conifer-dominated woodland where the landscape changes frequently.

Maturing trees lend appeal to much of the site, as a walk along the good network of paths reveals. A programme of felling and replanting brings

regular changes to the area.

In the valley the woodland is fairly open and pleasant to walk through.

Tucked away on the side of the valley are the oak woods of Porterthwaite where coarse Eskdale granite gives the hillside a rocky feel and the wood floor is clothed in mossy boulders, ferns and carpets of bilberry. On the edge of this section a delightful packhorse bridge crosses the river.

The woodland is dissected by miniature fern-lined ravines, cut by becks as they tumble down towards the river. This is a particularly lovely area of woodland – equally good for a quiet stroll or as part of a longer expedition.

MAP 1

Giggle Alley
Eskdale Green

Follow signs to Eskdale Green
from A595. The wood is just past
Eskdale Green post office and
stores. (NY142001)
9ha (22acres)
Forestry Commission

Once part of the Gatehouse
estate, the star attraction today
is the hidden Japanese Garden
created by the owner in 1914
and designed by Thomas
Mawson, the foremost
landscape architect of the day.

Featuring a lily pond, arched bridges, pavilion and narrow,
stone-surfaced paths the garden
was abandoned in 1949. Now
enclosed by woodland, visitors
feel as if they have discovered a
secret garden set in a hollow
on the top of the fell. The
beautiful spreading maples with
their brilliant autumn foliage
create a stunning display.

Since 1999 volunteers have
been working hard to clear
paths and steps and halt the
advance of invasive
rhododendrons and bamboos.

A leaflet describing the
history and restoration of the
gardens is available at the
Eskdale village stores.

Stanley Ghyll
Eskdale Green

Follow signs to Eskdale Green
from A595. Just beyond village turn
left towards Boot and 400m (0.25
mile) past the Beckfoot Halt Hotel
take the small turn right to Trough
House Bridge (war memorial on
right). Car park on left past bridge.
(NY171003)
9ha (22acres)
**Lake District National
Park Authority**

Short but dramatic, easy but
exciting, a walk through the
woodland of Stanley Ghyll is
an experience everyone –
particularly children –
can enjoy.

Part of the Dalegarth
amenity woods, the site is
made up of contrasting oak
and conifers. A stand of
conifers marks the start of a
short but scenic walk through
the site.

The path follows the beck
up the valley to a small, steep-
sided gorge where water

tumbles over Eskdale granite in a series of falls and pools.

Though easy to tackle along established paths, care is needed towards the top of the gorge where paths narrow and the rocks can get slippery.

Visitors can incorporate Stanley Ghyll as part of a longer exploration of the Dalegarth estate. A footpath follows a lovely stretch of the River Esk toward the semi-natural woodland higher up the valley. A visit to the miniature railway which runs from Dalegarth to Ravenglass could add a further dimension.

Muncaster Estate
Ravenglass

Signposted from A595 coast road. (SD103965)
77ha (190acres)
Muncaster Estate

Family groups who remain undaunted by the prospect of a climb will find their exertions well rewarded on a visit to the Muncaster Estate, for the ornamental woodlands, set within the grounds of Muncaster Castle itself, provide miles of woodland walks with features to enthral everyone from the young child to the keen horticulturalist.

The woods stretch across hills, enjoying a wonderful position overlooking the valley and providing views across to the fells beyond.

Many of the woodlands have fine tree specimens to discover – including some huge southern beeches and impressive conifers, which add drama to the site.

Elsewhere in the castle grounds there is much to keep younger visitors amused, including owls and a Meadow Vole Maze.

Paths are rough, uneven and sometimes steep and can become boggy in wet weather – so boots are recommended for your visit.

MAP 1

Hardknott Forest
Broughton in Furness

Turn right off A595 from
Broughton, just before River
Duddon, signed Ulpha. Follow
signs to Ulpha then Seathwaite –
keep going towards Hardknott
pass – forest is on the left.
(SD234996)
629ha (1555acres) SSSI
Forestry Commission

Hardknott Forest is full of
variety – with open glades,
rocky heather, bracken-clad
crags, rides, streams, bogs and
dense woodland providing
striking contrasts.

Choose your route from
short circular walks along the
valley bottom and lower slopes
to longer, more strenuous

climbs to the open Harter Fell.
Take a breather here and enjoy
some beautiful views across the
Duddon Valley and north to
the central Lakeland fells.

The plantations are mainly
coniferous but there is an area
of sessile oak woodland near to
the River Duddon.

Behind the evolution of the
site is a careful programme of
planting by the Forestry
Commission which began in
the 1940s and has evolved
through close talks with
foresters, the National Trust and
Friends of the Lake District.

The resulting mixture is
more varied and attractive than
many older Lake District
plantations and can be enjoyed
as part of a wider tour of other
woodlands in the valley such as
Rainsbarrow (see opposite).

Low Wood
Ulpha

On western slope of Duddon
Valley, southwest of the Lake
District National Park. (SD203943)
11ha (28acres) SSSI
The Woodland Trust

This ancient woodland is set
on steep slopes of the Duddon
Valley and is part of a large
series of woodland.

Oak, birch and sycamore
grow on the lower slopes of
the wood together with hazel,
holly and rowan. Higher up, on
land previously planted with
conifers, a young woodland of
oak, ash, alder, hazel, rowan and

holly is emerging.

The woodland floor holds plenty of interest. At one moment an abundance of knee-high ferns and the next, bluebell, violet and wild daffodil add a mass of spring colour. Look too for wood ant colonies which occur frequently throughout.

The site was previously managed through coppicing to provide wood for the local bobbin mills as well as charcoal for a forge and blast furnace at Duddon Bridge.

As the woodland is steep and rocky and has no formal paths, visitors are urged to take special care when exploring.

Rainsbarrow
Broughton in Furness

Turn off A595, turn right from Broughton, just before River Duddon, signed Ulpha. Follow signs to Ulpha. Rainsbarrow entrance by post office in village. (SD190926)
50ha (124acres) SSSI
Forestry Commission

Everyone, from the casual walker to the naturalist, can enjoy the wealth of discoveries awaiting them in Rainsbarrow wood.

A typical Lake District woodland mix of oak, ash, birch, elm and hazel, it has the additional bonus of offering lovely views across the Duddon Valley.

Children will find particular delight watching the wood ants, a species characteristic to the valley which nest in large numbers along the footpath, and if you take a circular walk through the wood up onto the open fell, you can enjoy a panorama of the Lake District fells, stretching south to Morecambe Bay.

A management programme by the Forestry Commission, which includes thinning and coppicing, is restoring the diversity of the woods and conserving the array of ground flora – among them bluebells, ramsons and primroses.

The woodland route follows narrow paths and wide rides which can get muddy. As with nearby Hardknott Forest, boots are recommended.

MAP 1

Grizedale Forest Park

Hawkshead

From the North: A591 to Ambleside, leave Ambleside A593 to Langdale/Coniston. First left B5286 to Hawkshead. By-pass Hawkshead follow B5286 south, first right, tourist sign 'Theatre in the Forest', follow to Grizedale approx. 3km (2 miles). From the South: M6 junction 36 take A591. First exit A590, Barrow follow A590 past Newby Bridge Haverthwaite crossroads, turn right, Tourist signs 'Grizedale Forest Park', follow signs for Satterthwaite/Grizedale. (SD335945)
2447ha (6048acres)

Forestry Commission

Situated between the lakes of Coniston and Windermere, Grizedale Forest Park provides a perfect introduction to anyone looking for their first woodland experience.

Extending to almost 12 square miles, this former timber plantation is set within a delightful Lakeland valley and is the largest forest within the Lake District. It is managed by the Forestry Commission for the benefit of wildlife and for visitors who can enjoy a range of recreational activities including cycle routes and orienteering courses.

While maturing conifers dominate, there are areas of indigenous hardwoods including sessile oak, birch and rowan. Wildlife includes red and roe deer and a variety of birds such as woodcocks, nightjars, pied flycatchers, green woodpeckers and buzzards.

Delightful sculptures, sited throughout, were created by artists working in residence at Grizedale and made the forest internationally famous. It would take several days to see all the works of art. However, a series of well-marked routes of varying degrees of difficulty allow visitors to discover these at a pace that suits them best.

Visitors flock to enjoy the miles of footpaths, forest rides and an all-ability trail, but the forest is successful in absorbing them unobtrusively.

There is a visitor centre with gallery, artist workshops, cafe, adventure playground, cycle hire facility and information point. A presentation in the visitor centre depicts the story of the forest from wildwood to the various roles it plays today.

There is a theatre in the forest that presents a wide range of events ranging from dance, classical and jazz music, drama, variety shows and folk concerts.

MAP 1

Claife Woods

Claife Woods
Hawkshead

Either approach on the B5285 Hawkshead to Windermere Ferry road, National Trust car park at foot of Ferry Hill or via road from High Wray village to the lake, car park at Red Nab. (SD385995) 230ha (568acres)

The National Trust

Set atop a hillside overlooking Windermere, Claife Woods is a large mixed woodland with panoramic views.

The walking is good and the woodland attractive and varied. On the lower slopes are dense woods where you will encounter oak, birch, alder, holly and yew with some stands of larch.

Higher up these give way to a patchwork of more open areas where Scots pine grow on the thin soil of the rocky knolls. Here, the landscape is dotted with small mires and tarns.

An extensive network of footpaths runs throughout, allowing visitors to choose between an easy route along the shore of the lake to the more strenuous which lead to a viewpoint at the summit at Claife Heights.

Skelghyll Wood
Ambleside

800m (0.5 mile) south of Ambleside on A591, turn left up to Stagshaw Gardens. (NY380028)
38ha (94acres)
The National Trust

A small, tumbling beck accompanies the rocky path as it climbs through the trees, finally emerging at Jenkyn's Crag, a rocky outcrop overlooking Windermere. Wonderful views of the Lake District make this a favourite picnic spot.

The lower part of the wood has many fine mature specimen trees including Wellingtonia, spruce and Douglas fir along with some large mature oak trees.

This wood makes a lovely short stroll with the reward of expansive views for those who make it to the top. It can also be used to gain access to the lower fells and a longer walk.

Rayrigg Wood
Windermere

The wood is east of the A592, north of Windermere. (SD404975)
14ha (35acres)
Pattinsons (Windermere) Ltd.

Sheriff's Walk provides an enjoyable stroll between the southern boundary of the wood and a small stream flowing through a rocky ghyll. Flowing over several small waterfalls, the stream is very picturesque.

Mainly oak with ash, birch and holly, further along is a fine glade of beech with its woodland floor burnished with bronze as the leaves come tumbling down in autumn. This area contrasts dramatically with the rest of the wood.

Look for the very large multi-stemmed sycamore along the boundary, most likely a remnant of an old laid hedge.

Probably created as a 'walk' during Victorian times, this makes a pleasant diversion from the busy streets of Bowness.

MAP 2

Ambleside   Skelghyll Wood p
Miterdale Forest p35   Hardknott   Beckmickle
Giggle Alley p36   Forest p38   Rayrigg   Ing p46
Muncaster Estate   Stanley   Wood
p37   Ghyll p36   Coniston   A593   Windermere
Low Wood p38   Claife Woods p
Rainsbarrow p39   Grizedale Forest   Kendal
  Park p40   Chapel
  House p52
Rusland Woods p46
Moss & Height Spring Wood p47   Witherslack   Brigste
Haverthwaite Heights p48   Wood p50   Park p5
  Brown Robin p49   Crag
Millom   Eggerslack   Wood
  Ulverston   Wood p50   p50
  Grange-   Arnside   1
Sea Wood p48   over-   Knott   2
  Sands   p57
  Warton Crag p58
  Carnfo
Barrow-in-Furness
  Morecambe
1   Gait Barrows NNR p54
2   Eaves Wood p58   Vicarage Wood p61
3   Hyning Scout Wood p60   Heysham   Lancas

N

10 miles
10 km

Fleetwood
  Garstang

A585

Blackpool
  Kirkham   Pre
Lytham St Anne's   Warton

4   Lever Park p82
5   Wilderswood p86   Cuerden Valley Pa
6   Walker Fold Woodlands p85   Leyla
7   High Shores Clough Woodland p86   Mere Sands
8   Raveden Wood, Smithills Hall Estate p88   Wood p76

MAP 3 ▼ (see p74)

Southport

44

Richmond

NORTH YORKSHIRE

A685

A683

A6108

Sedbergh

A684

Hawes

Leyburn

A6108

Kirkby
Lonsdale

MAP I ▲(see p18)

A687

A683

Thornton &
Twisleton Glens p62

*Yorkshire
Dales*

A65

Lower Grass
Wood p66

Settle

Scaleber Wood p65

*orest of
owland*

A65

A59

burn Forest p64

A682

Skipton Woods p68

Skipton

Ilkley

ANCASHIRE

A59

A682

A56

A629

acon Fell
untry Park p72

Keighley

Clitheroe

Bingley

Hagg
Wood
p70

A6068

A650

ring Wood p71

Colne

13

Shipley

A59

12

Nelson

M65

A6033

A629

ove Lane Plantations p70

Burnley

11

10

BRADFORD

8

9

7

8

Towneley
Woods p69

Hardcastle
Crags p67

A6036

lackburn

6

Accrington

M65

Halifax

M606

Roddlesworth &
Tockholes Woods p73

Rawtenstall

Todmorden

26

A675

A666

A56

Brighouse

25

A671

A58

24

ley

5

6

7

8

Jumbles Country
Park p87

Rochdale

22

M62

23

Huddersfield

M66

21

A62

45

MAP 2

Beckmickle Ing
Burneside

On the bank of the River Kent, just east of the village of Staveley, near Kendal. (SD490979)
4ha (9acres) SSSI
The Woodland Trust

Birdsong, bluebells and beauty – Beckmickle Ing, on the banks of the River Kent, has it all.

This is a well-loved ancient woodland site on the border of the Lake District National Park, as popular with visitors as with locals. A visit here can be combined with one of many walk routes in the area, including the Dalesway long-distance path.

Inside the wood, where roe deer roam and the red squirrel is occasionally spotted, is a rich mix of broadleaves and a wonderfully diverse range of ground flora. Take in the sights and smells of ramson, lords-and-ladies, moschatel, pignut and Solomon's seal.

On the banks of the river, in which nationally important crayfish and mussel populations live, are rushes, hemlock, water-dropwort and the yellow globeflower.

If you are lucky you might spot resident great spotted woodpeckers or spy dippers and common sandpipers around the river and bank.

Rusland Woods
Newby Bridge

From A590 take turning signposted Grizedale/Rusland. Follow signs for approx. 3km (2 miles). Rusland Woods on right – lookout for LDNP sign. (SD335893)
60ha (148acres)
Lake District National Park Authority

Wonderfully atmospheric, Rusland Woods is a lovely site to explore.

A rich mix of mainly open broadleaved trees, with handsome, mature examples dotted throughout, it looks as good in the mist and rain as it does on bright days with sun filtering through the canopy.

Beech, yew and oak dominate the woodland and one wonderful old sweet chestnut stands near the entrance gate. Further up the hill a beautiful mature spreading oak adds drama to an already feature-packed walk.

The path, while not surfaced, makes for easy walking and is well marked with white-topped posts.

The famous Rusland beeches line the road along the edge of the woods. Many of the ancient trees remain, although some have been felled and replanted to secure the future of this attractive feature.

Within the woodland, rocky outcrops run in parallel ridges up the hillside, forming small cliffs. Yew and occasionally beech trees cling to rocks, their roots snaking across the rock surface.

Moss & Height Spring Wood
Bouth

3km (2 miles) north of Bouth and A590, car park on left. (SD324863) 19ha (48acres)

The Woodland Trust

History is never far away in Moss & Height Spring Wood, near Ulverston in Cumbria.

The wood is believed to be at least 350 years old and the wide track that dissects it is considered an old coffin route used by the people of Bouth to reach the church at Colton.

Most of the oak-dominated wood today is mixed coppice including hazel, birch and alder, with oak standards and mature yew trees. Several small streams meander through, creating mossy and boggy areas, while more than 2,000 metres of footpath criss-cross this well-loved rural spot. The red squirrel is resident here.

A rich ground flora includes dog's mercury, bilberry, primrose, honeysuckle, violets and wild strawberry.

A conifer block in the west of Moss Wood has been replanted with native broadleaves, and birch allowed to re-seed naturally. This re-creation of native woodland is helping to restore the biodiversity of this ancient site.

MAP 2

Haverthwaite Heights
Grange-over-Sands / Ulverston

Turn northwards off A590 at
Haverthwaite crossroads,
signposted to Bouth/Rusland/
Grizedale, and then immediately
right along old road. (SD342845)
78ha (193acres)
**Lake District National
Park Authority**

Haverthwaite Heights is a rich
and interesting mix of ancient
woodland set atop craggy,
undulating hillside in south
Lakeland.

The higher sections of the
woodland, topped with lovely
gnarled mature Scots pine, are
particularly attractive.

A short but delightful walk
along a hillside path takes
visitors up through the wood.

Although steep in places, the
going is not too difficult with
plenty of chances to enjoy
panoramic views over
Morecambe Bay.

En route you encounter
areas of mature larch and
former conifer plantations now
largely replanted with native
broadleaves. Much of the site
has broadleaf cover, with old
oak coppice, birch and yew.
Bracken, foxgloves and
bluebells can be found on the
woodland floor and as you
climb higher you find
bilberry too.

If you want to explore
further, a permissive path
through the wood to
Backbarrow provides a circular
walk and you can even take a
trip along the valley on the
Haverthwaite railway.

Sea Wood
Bardsea

On the northwest shore of
Morecambe Bay, approximately
5km (3 miles) south of Ulverston
at Bardsea. (SD293734)
23ha (58acres) SSSI
The Woodland Trust

A trip to the seaside can take
on new meaning with a visit to
Sea Wood. The woodland stands
out against the northwest shore
of Morecambe Bay and is
edged by the shingle beach of
Ulverston Sands.

The sea played an important
part in the management of the
wood – large oak timbers used

to be floated at high tide to ship builders in Ulverston.

Today this semi-natural ancient woodland is something of a county rarity and is recognised as the largest of its kind in South Cumbria.

Notable for its many old oak trees, the site is a rich broadleaf mix while the ground vegetation, denser in the northern wood, supports a host of small mammals. There is also a thriving population of small birds, blackbirds and thrushes. Look for the many types of lichen that add texture and colour to the tree trunks.

Brown Robin
Grange-over-Sands

From mini roundabout near Grange over Sands railway station take B5271, access to reserve is 1km (0.75 mile) on right.
(SD411783)
13ha (32acres)
Cumbria Wildlife Trust

Evenly split between grassland and woodland, Brown Robin reserve is rich in wildlife and a pleasure to explore.

The woods are at their most spectacular in spring when bluebells, ramsons, wild daffodils and primroses carpet the floor. Hart's tongue fern and dog's mercury are also seen growing here.

Interest is amplified by the mosaic of habitats that make up this site – from sunny open grassland to deep, shady wood. Stop off at one of a number of great picnic spots and take time to observe the array of wildlife including roe deer, woodpeckers and buzzards.

The underlying limestone bedrock has produced a distinctive mix of dominant ash, hazel and yew with oak, beech, sycamore and elm.

Walking is fairly easy and the paths, which range from farm tracks to narrow winding woodland routes lead to the top of the reserve from where panoramic views across Morecambe Bay can be enjoyed.

MAP 2

Eggerslack Wood
Grange-over-Sands

Turn off A590 south onto B5271
towards Grange. Wood is
approx.1.6km (1 mile) on right.
(SD408784)
47ha (116acres)
Forestry Commission

Good paths lead through
predominantly mixed
broadleaved woodland where
you wander between birch,
ash, oak, holly, rowan, yew and
areas of hazel coppice. There
are also planted areas of beech,
larch and sycamore.

At the bottom of the wood is
a peaceful, shady hazel coppice.
Along the path the wood opens
out and sun slips through the
canopy of oak, birch, ash and
sycamore revealing dog's
mercury and ferns.

Up the hill, limestone
outcrops support common dog
violet, bluebell and woodrush
and, at the top, open grassland
makes a wonderful picnic spot
with panoramic views across
Morecambe Bay.

Gently descend through
woods of wild cherry and ash
and oak. The path passes a lovely
mature oak and a wonderfully
clear spring on the way down.

Crag Wood
Meathop

On the edge of Morecambe Bay
estuary in the Lake District
National Park. (SD457806)
4ha (9acres)
The Woodland Trust

Precipitous limestone cliffs drop
dramatically down to the
mudflats below. In the middle
of the woodland a seasonal
pond with yellow iris, bulrush
and soft rush and edged with

alder and willow attracts birdlife
including mallard, heron,
sparrowhawk, chiff-chaff,
willow warbler and goldcrest.

Oak, birch, ash and cherry
are all to be found in this
ancient woodland. Keep your
eye out too for the occasional
mature yew tree. Beneath this
canopy is a mix of hazel,
hawthorn, blackthorn, holly
and crab apple.

The woodland floor comes
alive each spring with a fine
display of bluebells and wood
anemones. Yorkshire fog,

Frosted Holly

wood-sorrel, bugle and yellow pimpernel add their colour amongst trailing honeysuckle and bramble.

Access can be gained from the Cumbria Coastal Way to the north of the wood.

Witherslack Wood
Witherslack / Lindale

From A590 turn off and follow signs to Witherslack. Continue north on minor road for approx.1.6km (1 mile) to Witherslack Hall. (SD433862) 400ha (989acres) SSSI

The Stanley Family

An extensive and varied area of woodland with distinct woodland characters from sheltered, sunny glades to exposed limestone scree.

Where woodland grows above siliceous rocks you will find fine, mature oaks. Contrast this with the nearby limestone woodland of ash, yew and hazel coppice. Look for lovely stunted birch trees on the hillsides and the extensive views beyond.

Perhaps best explored as part of a longer walk whilst taking in surrounding areas such as Whitbarrow Scar or parking at Low Fell End. An OS map is recommended for exploring this area.

51

MAP 2

Chapel House
Newby Bridge

Head north on A592 towards
Windermere from A590 at Newby
Bridge. After 1.6km (1 mile) turn
right and head up hill for a further
1km. Parking is on the right. The
car park is signed Gummer's How.
Turn off A590 at sign to Staveley.
Park on lay-by along minor road
from where there is access to the
plantation via a forest ride.
(SD397875)
333ha (823acres)
Forestry Commission

Despite its name, this is a large
mixed coniferous plantation.
Yet it is alive with such small
birds as titmice, treecreepers
and goldcrests.

The car park at the top end
is used by walkers who follow
a permissive path through the
woods to begin their ascent of
Gummer's How. For something
less strenuous, there's a short
circular walk that returns via
the road to the car park.

Park at the bottom of the
hill and there are a number of
public footpaths – some
following forest rides –
through the wood. The
walking is easy and the paths
lead up through well-thinned
larch plantations with
wonderful views across
Windermere and the fells.

A reservoir within the wood,
areas of open fell, rocky
outcrops and scattered oaks
festooned with mosses and
ferns all add variety.

Brigsteer Park
Levens Village

Follow signs from A590 to Levens
village. Pass through village and
follow signs to Brigsteer. Wood is
approx. 2.5km (1.5 miles) after
Levens village. (SD488876)
34ha (83acres)
The National Trust

Mrs Humphry Ward brought
Brigsteer Park to the attention
of Victorians through her novel
Hellbeck of Bannisdale,
describing its magnificent
daffodil display as being 'flung
on the fellside through a score
of acres'. You don't have to
restrict visits to the spring as
Brigsteer is a joy any time
of year.

Hazelnuts

Set on a limestone hillside overlooking the Lyth valley, this site provides a rich habitat for birds, plants and insects – including butterflies – with plenty to offer the woodland walker, whatever the season.

Splendid old yews intermix with oak, ash, hazel and holly with underplanted beech and conifers now being thinned by the National Trust in a bid to restore a more natural balance. Overgrown hazel is being re-coppiced and felled timber is left to rot to provide new habitats for insects.

A network of wide tracks and narrow winding paths provide ample opportunities to explore, with wonderful views over the Lyth valley and its renowned damson orchards.

MAP 2

Gait Barrows National Nature Reserve
Silverdale

From A6 follow signs to Leighton Moss RSPB reserve. After passing reserve turn right at T-junction past Silverdale station and continue, ignoring minor road to left and road to right, over railway line, turning left to Waterslack after approx 1km (0.75 mile). Entrance to Gait Barrows 1.6km (1 mile) on right. (SD478773)

117ha (289acres) AONB, SSSI

Natural England

Gait Barrows National Nature Reserve

Casual visitors and naturalists alike will find plenty of interest at Gait Barrows National Nature Reserve – not least the views across the Arnside and Silverdale Area of Outstanding Natural Beauty.

This delightfully sheltered site boasts perhaps the country's finest example of limestone pavement supporting a miniature woodland of stunted yew, ash, elm, rowan

55

MAP 2

and hazel trees. These grow very slowly in the limestone cracks – known as 'grikes' – where root growth is restricted and water in short-supply – some of the trees may well be over 300 years old.

Two waymarked trails take the visitor gently through woodland, surrounding meadows, fen, reedbeds and to the lakes of Little Hawes Water and Hawes Water. This is easy walking but care should be taken on the limestone, particularly in wet conditions.

Rare butterflies, such as the high brown fritillary, pearl bordered fritillary and Duke of Burgundy, might be seen here. It is worth spending some time peering into the limestone grikes to discover the range of plantlife sheltering here. Among the many rarities are ferns and the dark-red helleborine.

Surrounding the open pavement are mixed woodland areas of oak and ash with a dense understorey of spindle, guelder rose, dogwood and hazel. Thrang Wood is a haunting area of ancient yew woodland littered with moss-covered boulders. Dark and cool, the wood is in startling contrast to the bright open pavement which slopes south and seems to radiate heat even on fairly overcast days.

An amazing 1,600 types of fungi and 800 species of moth have been recorded in these woods. Wood ants are common particularly in the north of the reserve. Birdlife includes such notable species as the bittern and marsh harrier.

While the best time to visit for flowering plants is during spring and summer months, year-round interest is provided by the reserve's variety of woodland birds.

Arnside Knott
Arnside, Carnforth

From A6 at Milnthorpe take B5282 and follow signs to Arnside and the Arnside Knott. (SD456775)
107ha (264acres) AONB, SSSI
The National Trust

There is a rich and varied landscape to explore on Arnside Knott, a 150m (500ft) limestone hill with stunning views across Morecambe Bay.

Noted for its rich flora and butterflies, you can explore several areas – each with its own distinctive character. Walking is easy through the mosaic of woodland, scrub and tussocky herb-rich grassland.

On the summit is a mixture of scrub and grassland, dotted with the weathered stumps of larch trees cut down in 1914, with views towards the Lakes.

Redhills Wood, clothing the northern slopes, has a maze of narrow paths and rides leading you through a dense mix of oak, hazel, holly and yew trees with violets and primroses in spring.

Further round the hill, the branches of splendid old yews cast deep shadows, while on the lower slopes more open, mixed oak woodland contrasts with Redhills.

Circular walks can be extended to take in nearby sites of interest such as neighbouring Heathwaite.

Arnside Knott

MAP 2

Eaves Wood
Silverdale

From A6 follow signs to Leighton Moss RSPB reserve. Continue past reserve on left and take right turn at T-junction. Drive past Silverdale station on the right and continue along road to Eaves Wood car park, approx I km (0.75 mile). (SD465758)
43ha (106acres) AONB, SSSI
The National Trust

Eaves Wood is a delightful mix of ancient coppice woodland, limestone and Victorian amenity woods.

Children can enjoy discovering a circle of trees known as the Ring o' Beeches, a stone tower called the Pepper Pot overlooking Morecambe Bay – built for Queen Victoria's golden jubilee – and the ruins of Emes Cottage, a former woodcutter's home.

A network of paths through the site meanders across open areas of limestone, then plunges into dense ancient woodland. Flowering plants, lichens and insects associated with ancient woodland thrive here. Moss- and fern-covered limestone outcrops emerge in parallel ridges across the woodland floor.

Tall Scots pines reach high into the canopy while beech trees spread wide over a clear woodland floor, turning it golden each autumn.

Higher up, limestone areas are home to a host of rare species including the dark-red helleborine and bloody cranesbill and rare butterflies such as the pearl bordered fritillary.

Warton Crag
Carnforth

From junction 35A on M6 take A6 north. First left to Warton village and left at crossroads in main street. Right into Crag Road, at George Washington pub, main car park 500m on right. (SD493728)
35ha (87acres) AONB, SSSI
Lancashire Wildlife Trust

Records show that man first settled on Warton Crag as long ago as the first century. It is easy to understand why.

From the summit of the crag there are breathtaking views across Morecambe Bay. The woods themselves are full of

Warton Crag

variety and interest – switching from dense shady woodland dotted with moss-covered boulders and ferns to open sunny clearings over a limestone pavement.

Thanks to the good network of paths, you could spend hours exploring the hillside and woods.

The southern slopes are clothed in species-rich grassland and scrub while the woodlands are dominated by ash with hazel, oak, birch and the occasional yew. The remains of semi-circular ramparts north of the summit are thought to have been once part of a hill fort.

Spring and early summer see the woods carpeted with colourful flora and filled with butterflies – including the rare high brown fritillary. Summer visitors are serenaded by an orchestra of warblers, including chiff-chaffs, whitethroats and blackcaps.

MAP 2

Hyning Scout Wood
Yealand Conyers

Lies between Yealand Conyers and
Warton, approximately 8km (5
miles) west of Junction 35 of M6.
(SD501735)
21ha (52acres) AONB
The Woodland Trust

A place of beauty and
atmosphere, you can stroll
beneath wonderful big beech
and sweet chestnuts dating
back maybe 200 years with
delightful spring carpets of
bluebells at your feet.

Much is ancient woodland –
a mixture of mature ash,
sycamore, sweet chestnut and
oak that has evolved on the
clints (limestone blocks) and
grikes (water-eroded gaps) of
the Arnside and Silverdale Area
of Outstanding Natural Beauty.

Rare ferns and flowers found
here include the downy currant
and the rigid buckler fern. Red
squirrels can still be seen around
Hyning and browsing roe deer
are often spotted.

The remains of a limestone
kiln can be seen in the south of
the wood. Today the limestone
is legally protected from
excavation and damage.

Many well-used footpaths
provide good circular walks and
link up with routes across
neighbouring countryside. Care
should be taken on the
limestone pavements which can
become slippery when wet.

Hyning Scout Wood

Vicarage Wood
Morecambe

Leave M6 at junction 34, follow signs for Heysham then brown tourist signs for St Patrick's Chapel. Park in pay-and-display car park in Heysham Village. (SD410617)
2ha (5acres)
The National Trust

Tiny Vicarage Wood was planted in the 19th century in an idyllic coastal headland setting, overlooking picture postcard Heysham.

Despite its size, the woodland is packed with charm, character and history. It is a great place for children to explore, too.

Many small paths wind through the wood, where bluebells and red campion adorn the woodland floor in spring and early summer. Exposed low cliffs and massive sandstone boulders add drama and atmosphere.

The sycamore-dominated wood offers shelter from the sea breezes that sweep across Morecambe Bay and makes a wonderful contrast with the neighbouring open headland. Many trees on the seaward side have been stunted by the wind.

There is evidence of human activity dating back thousands of years. Indeed, the headland is one of Lancashire's most important archaeological sites and the wood itself houses a rock-cut grave, probably linked to an early Christian site near the ruins of an old chapel on the cliffs.

MAP 2

Thornton & Twisleton Glens

Ingleton

On the edge of Ingleton village parking is provided for the Waterfalls Walk (signposted) by the Ingleton Scenery Company, a charge is made for the parking and access to the woodlands. (SD695750 and SD700742)

8ha (20acres) SSSI

The Woodland Trust

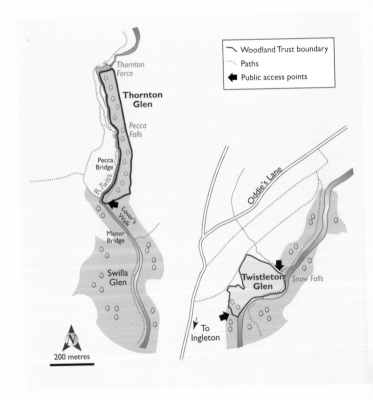

Ancient woodland is something of a rarity in North Yorkshire making Thornton & Twisleton Glens all the more valuable.

Situated on the banks of the River Twiss and River Doe, the two woods are part of a larger unbroken chain of ancient woodland following each river's course in the Yorkshire Dales National Park.

Ingleton had been known for its caves and mountain scenery since the second half of the 18th century, but the now famous waterfalls of the Ingleton Glens were hidden in tree-filled craggy ravines. So difficult were they to get to that even the farmers and quarrymen who earned their living nearby were unaware of their existence.

Both woods are accessed via the stunningly beautiful 7km (4.5 mile) Waterfalls Walk from Ingleton. Since the late 19th century, visitors have enjoyed this route, which includes ancient oak woodland, geological features and magnificent Dales scenery.

The walk leads you through spectacular landscapes of dramatic outcrops with cascades and waterfalls – the most famous being Thornton Force. There is a viewing area here where you can enjoy a picnic and watch the river fall 14 metres (45ft) over limestone rocks in an impressive cascade. Also, don't miss Snow Falls beside Twisleton Glen. Look out for lichens and soft mosses that thrive in the deep dark gullies.

The rock steps into which these glens have cut were formed as a result of the different resistance to erosion of the rocks lying each side of the great earth fractures known as the Craven Faults.

While visitors today will enjoy the rich mosaic of plants that cover Twisleton's woodland floor, a profusion of wild ferns, lilies of the valley and wild orchids once grew here. Unfortunately these were dug up during the 19th and 20th centuries and sold as souvenirs to visitors.

MAP 2

Gisburn Forest

Gisburn Forest
Settle / Clitheroe

Take A65 east towards Leeds, at
Long Preston take B6478 south to
Slaidburn. After approx.11km
(7 miles) take right-hand turning to
Gisburn (between Tosside and
Slaidburn). From west on A65 take
turning signposted Clapham
Station, Keasden near village of
Clapham. Follow minor road
across Clapham Moor to Forest.
(SD745551 & SD733565)
1236ha (3055acres) AONB
Forestry Commission

Although Gisburn Forest is in
a fairly remote location,
surrounded by open

countryside, it is well worth
the effort to get there –
particularly if you are a keen
naturalist or birdwatcher.

The expansive, mainly
coniferous forest on the edge
of the Stocks Reservoir is one
of the best wildfowl sites in the
northwest – red-breasted
merganser breed here.

Easy strolls can be enjoyed
along one of several
waymarked trails, cycleways
and bridleways – with lots of
potential picnic spots.

Much of the plantation is
being harvested and the variety
of young and mature trees
provide various habitats.
Visitors may find interest in

the replanted and regenerating broadleaf areas.

Park Wood, an area of semi-natural woodland along Bottoms Beck, is particularly good for plants and insects. Water tumbles along the beck while inside the woodland you might spot titmice, finches and even crossbills. The open rides support a lovely variety of flora including early purple and spotted orchid.

Scaleber Wood
Settle

From Settle follow High Hill Lane southeast. A small area for parking directly adjacent to wood. (SD840625)
4ha (10acres), SSSI
The Woodland Trust

A real people magnet, Scaleber Wood in the heart of the Yorkshire Dales packs a powerful mix of breathtaking sights and evocative sounds into a small space.

The most spectacular is Scaleber Force, a stunning 12 metre (40ft) waterfall whose crystal waters tumble over limestone cliffs before plunging into a deep pool.

The site lies on the Elgar Way — named after the great English composer who was a regular visitor — a 21km (13 mile) circular walk from Settle that takes in impressive crags, gorges and waterfalls.

Scaleber Wood lies within the Attermire Scar, Site of Special Scientific Interest for its remarkable limestone geology with huge rocky outcrops and associated flora.

The wood itself, a mix of broadleaves and planted conifers, is tricky to access and taxing to explore, but the spectacular sight of the waterfall only a short walk from the road.

MAP 2

Lower Grass Wood
Grassington

From Grassington follow Grass
Wood Lane north and park where
there are a number of lay-bys and
a small, Yorkshire Wildlife Trust car
park. (SD983651)
8.5ha (21acres)

The Woodland Trust

Ancient woodland adorns
this stretch of the River
Wharfe valley less than a
mile from Grassington.

This linear mixed broadleaf
site is an important part of
one of the Yorkshire Dales
National Park's largest ancient
woodland areas.

The wood has an open
character, due to the loss of
most of the elm trees, with a
light canopy of sycamore, oak,
ash and birch with occasional
larch and beech. But Nature is
plugging the gaps with dense
patches of regenerating
hawthorn, birch, beech and ash.

A wealth of colourful flowers
includes carpets of bluebells
and dog's mercury, orchids
during summer, and rich

Lower Grass Wood

carpets of herbs on the steep open riverside slopes. Two 'elling hearths', small stone-lined pits used to produce potash, can be seen here.

Extend your visit by crossing the road to Yorkshire Wildlife Trust's Grass Wood and climb toward open ground at its summit. An extensive programme of restoration work is returning this wood to its former glory.

Hardcastle Crags
Hebden Bridge

Take A6033 (Keighley Road) north of Hebden Bridge. Turn left into Midgehole Road, follow to the end into National Trust car park. (SD988295)

125ha (309acres)

The National Trust

A dramatic landscape and interesting history join forces at Hardcastle Crags to forge an attractive woodland of interest to all ages.

Over the years the steep wooded valley of Hebden Gorge has supported a range of industries – wool from local farms supplied the textile mill in the valley, while charcoal burners provided fuel for local iron smelting.

Today the steep-sided gorge is clothed in beech, sycamore, oak, birch, larch and Scots pine, planted over 150 years. Woodrush, ferns, bracken and bluebells cover the ground where thousands of wood ants rustle through the foliage.

Look out for the slurring stone – a large rock where local children used to slide in their clogs, and an old pannier route that winds up the hillside.

A choice of walks includes the chance to climb the hillside towards Hardcastle Crags, the rocky outcrops that give the woods their name. Boots are recommended, particularly for anyone venturing onto the open moors.

MAP 2

Skipton Woods
Skipton

From Skipton town centre car park at rear of town hall (pay-and-display) follow Springs Canal towpath to woods' main entrance. (SD990525)

15ha (37acres)

The Woodland Trust

A magical land in the heart of town – that's one way to describe Skipton Woods, a woodland haven by one of Britain's best-preserved, most-popular medieval castles.

The woods' links with the castle date back at least 1,000 years. A canal towpath, following the line of Skipton Castle ramparts and Springs Canal, provides a direct link between the town's High Street and the woods, following the course of Eller Beck through a stunning steep-sided valley.

Most of this ancient woodland is dominated by ash but the occasional sycamore, beech, Scots pine, Norway spruce and hornbeam indicate a greater variety in the past. The woods are renowned for their vivid displays of bluebells and wild garlic and sustain five species of bat. Green and great spotted woodpeckers add their colour, while kingfisher and heron may be seen fishing the waterways

In 1998 the Woodland Trust resurfaced 2000 metres of paths to allow much easier access.

Skipton Woods

Towneley Woods
Burnley

Follow signs from M65 & A671 for
Towneley Hall Park. (SD855307)
20ha (49acres)

Burnley Borough Council

Woodland has existed in the
grounds of historic Towneley
Hall since 1400, but the
visitor's route is along paths
laid out in the 1800s when the
grounds were landscaped in
classic English style.

The legacy of this historical
background can be enjoyed
among the mixed native
broadleaves and exotic species
that populate the site today.
Look for sculptures created
along the walks here and at
nearby Grove Lane Plantations,
Padiham (see next page) and in
the woods of Gawthorpe Hall.

Towering beech trees are a
feature of this woodland. The
many other surprises waiting
to be discovered include relics
from the 19th century such as
an arched passageway in
Thanet Lee Wood, a ha-ha,
rustic tunnels and the Monks'
Well grotto.

The woodland itself is a
mixture of exotic and native
trees. Soil changes throughout
the site are reflected in the
variety of ground flora –
clay-loving ramson in some
sections contrasting with an
abundance of bluebells in
more acidic areas.

MAP 2

Hagg Wood
Ightenhill

Junction 10 on M65, turn down
Ightenhill Park Lane and park
100m before lane ends, in lay-by.
Cross Woodland Trust marked
stile, just before lane continues
through gate as bridleway.
(SD817346)
5ha (14acres)
The Woodland Trust

Ancient woodland sites such as
Hagg Wood are rare in
Lancashire.

Set in an open landscape
of sheep-grazed grassland,
moors and hills, this provides
an important wildlife haven.
The wood also extends
down a steep bank to the
River Calder.

Packed into this small wood
are many distinct areas. In the
heart of the wood young
birch, oak, rowan, holly and
sycamore are regenerating,
surrounded by a fringe of older
mature broadleaves.

Of the colourful variety of
flowering plants to be found
here, bluebell, wood anemone,
honeysuckle and enchanter's
nightshade indicate this is
indeed ancient woodland.
Meadowsweet, giant horsetail,
cuckoo pint and a variety of
ferns add to the wood's
undoubted appeal. Jay,
sparrowhawk, little owl and
kingfisher have been spotted
in the wood or down by
the river.

There is good public access
from Ightenhill Park Lane and
an attractive circular walk.

Grove Lane Plantations
Padiham

Follow cycleway signs from A671
roundabout via Lune Street,
Holmes Street, Ingham Street &
Grove Lane. (SD800343)
7ha (17acres)
Burnley Borough Council

This lovely airy wood, boasting
some magnificent old trees,
young woodland and fine,
south-facing views across
meadows, is well loved and
cared for so that visitors are
made to feel welcome.

The route of a tramway or
ginny which once served the
local coal mining industry, now
provides a flat, all-access path.

This forms part of a 'trail of words' with handrail carvings and words by local schoolchildren. Keep your eye out for a woodpecker carved out of a beech stump elsewhere in the wood.

Green and great spotted woodpeckers, nuthatches and tawny owls plus daubenton, pipistrelle and brown long-eared bats are all found here. Bluebells, wood anemone, red campion and ramson grow beneath an attractive broadleaf mix of beech, sycamore, oak, ash, rowan, birch and hazel. Young oak trees are starting to establish, as well as ash, holly, hazel and alder within new glades.

Spring Wood
Whalley

Immediately adjacent to A671 Whalley by-pass. Signposted Spring Wood Picnic Site. (SD741361) 16ha (40acres)

Lancashire County Council

A gentle climb through this historic, broadleaved wood leads to a bracken-clad summit offering panoramic views over the surrounding countryside.

Originally owned by the monks of Whalley Abbey, it once formed part of a deer park known as Oxheyewoode which was sold in 1553 along with other abbey lands. The presence of rhododendron, planted during the 19th century, indicates game cover for pheasant and woodcock.

There has been much planting on the site so that today the wood contains a mix of oak, ash, beech and sycamore growing above fine spring displays of bluebells and ransoms. Large beech trees accompany your approach to the summit where two fine specimens frame the panoramic view of Longridge Fell and Waddington Fell.

There is a good network of paths throughout and most are well surfaced.

MAP 2

Beacon Fell
Country Park
Chipping

Signposted from A6 north of
Preston. (SD565427)
87ha (215acres) AONB
Lancashire County Council

Set atop an isolated hill 266
metres (873ft) above sea level,
this country park is popular
with visitors who turn up in
large numbers.

Despite this, it is easy to find
a quiet walk or picnic spot on
open moorland or in
woodland clearings.

A variety of trees frame
wonderful panoramic views
from the Fell. Conifers used to
dominate but these have been
thinned and replanted, allowing
rowan, birch, alder and oak to
emerge, and creating habitats
for a rich variety of wildlife.

What makes this a delight to
explore is the contrast between
enclosed cool and shady
plantations – with their subtle
interplay of light and shadow –
and the sunny stretches of open
moorland. Wonderful in sunshine,
it has interest even when the fell
is shrouded in mist.

The site has something for
everyone from gentle walking
along a network of paths to
mountain biking, orienteering
and a sculpture trail to
amuse children.

Cuerden Valley Park
Bamber Bridge

South of Preston, easy access
from junctions 28 and 29 on M6.
Follow brown tourist signs.
(SD565238)
260ha (643acres)
Cuerden Valley Park Trust

Set within the valley of the
River Lostock, visitors can
enjoy a variety of landscapes
from woodland young and old
to lush grazing pastures, a lake,
ponds and the river.

Near the Hall the woodlands
feature oak, ash, sycamore,
hornbeam, yew, beech, Scots
pine and Chilean pine or
monkey puzzle, with some
impressively large trees to
be seen.

Bluebells carpet these woods
in spring and they provide a
good habitat for a number of
bird species.

A network of well-surfaced footpaths meanders through this attractive and extensive park making walking generally easy. The less-able can enjoy a level path from Town Brow to the picnic area near the lake. All kissing gates allow wheelchair access but choose your route carefully as, once inside the park, some paths are on steep ground and are stepped.

A few areas are provided as undisturbed refuges for wildlife and so restricted to visitors.

Roddlesworth & Tockholes Woods
Darwen

Take junction 3 off M65 and follow A675 towards Bolton. Approx. 4km (2.5 miles) after Abbey village turn sharp left down road signposted to Tockholes. Park at Visitor Centre near the Royal Arms. (SD665215) 195ha (482acres)
United Utilities

One of Lancashire's largest broadleaved woods, Roddlesworth includes such dramatic features as reservoirs, dark beech woods and attractive open moorland ideal for picnics.

Planted from 1904 by Liverpool Corporation to halt erosion of the valley sides, the site is dominated by a mix of oak, ash, beech, alder and pine. Today it is full of surprises, changing frequently – sometimes suddenly – from dense plantations of gnarled and twisted beech trees to open areas of oak and birch.

Don't be put off by rather uninspiring names: Tockholes Number Two plantation is more engaging than its title suggests. Bluebells adorn the woodland floor and scent the air in spring and in the autumn fungi are prolific.

A good network of paths, including several waymarked routes run through habitats that support great spotted woodpecker, goldcrest, treecreeeper and wood warbler while the small stream, flowing beneath small cliffs, draws dipper and kingfisher.

MAP 3

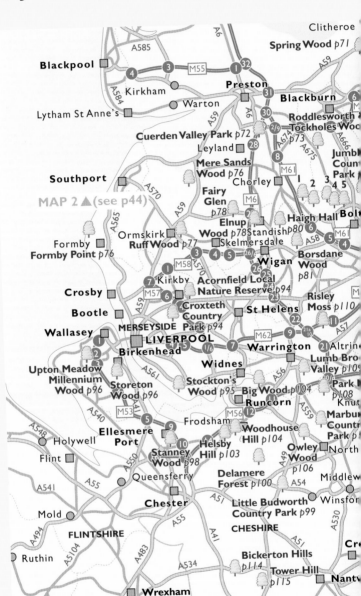

Clitheroe

Spring Wood p71

Blackpool

Kirkham

M55

Preston

Warton

Lytham St Anne's

Blackburn

Roddlesworth
Tockholes Woo
p73

Cuerden Valley Park p72

Leyland

Mere Sands
Wood p76

Southport

MAP 2 ▲ (see p44)

Fairy
Glen
p78

Chorley

Jumb
Coun
Park

Haigh Hall
p80

Bol

Formby
Formby Point p76

Ormskirk
Ruff Wood p77

Elnup
Wood p78 Standish

Skelmersdale

Wigan

Borsdane
Wood
p81

Crosby

Kirkby

Acornfield Local
Nature Reserve p94

Risley
Moss p110

Bootle

Croxteth
Country
Park p94

St Helens

Wallasey

LIVERPOOL

Birkenhead

Warrington

Altrin
Lumb Bro
Valley p109

Upton Meadow
Millennium
Wood p96

Widnes

Storeton
Wood p96

Stockton's
Wood p95

Big Wood p104

Runcorn

Park
p108

Knut

Marbu
Count
Park p

Ellesmere
Port

Holywell

Frodsham

Woodhouse
Hill p104

Owley
Wood
p106

North

Flint

Stanney
Wood p98

Helsby
Hill p103

Delamere
Forest p100

Middlew

Queensferry

Chester

Little Budworth
Country Park p99

Winsfor

Mold

CHESHIRE

FLINTSHIRE

Ruthin

Bickerton Hills
p114

Tower Hill
p115

Nantw

Cr

Wrexham

74

1 Lever Park p82
2 Wilderswood p86
3 Walker Fold Woodlands p85
4 High Shores Clough Woodland p86
5 Raveden Wood, Smithills Hall Estate p88

75

MAP 3

Formby Point
Formby

Turn off A565 onto B5424 and
follow brown tourist signs to
Formby Point. (SD275082)
209ha (517acres) SSSI

The National Trust

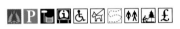

Sand, sea and squirrels are the
ingredients that make a visit to
Formby Point a unique
woodland experience. Tall
pines, planted in 1900, tower
above an undulating landscape
of old sand dunes.

Famous for its red squirrels –
descendents of the darker
continental species – these
delightfully bold creatures give
visitors the rare chance of a
close encounter. This is
especially fun for children who
can buy squirrel food from a
National Trust kiosk.

The pines are attractive and
well spaced, contrasting with
denser areas of scrubby
broadleaved woodland
consisting of birch, sycamore,
ash, oak and poplar. Open
grassland areas add to this
fascinating patchwork of
habitats. Closer to the sea,
trees give way to sand dunes
with marram grass and a sandy
beach beyond.

Walking is easy thanks to a
network of paths through the
plantation to the sea, some
providing circular walks. It is
usually dry underfoot so walking
boots are rarely needed.

Mere Sands Wood
Ormskirk

Leave A59 in Rufford village along
Holmewood Road, B5246. Reserve
entrance down drive 1.6km
(1 mile) on left. (SD447157)
42ha (104acres) SSSI

**Wildlife Trust for Lancashire,
Manchester & North Merseyside**

A woodland oasis in the flat
agricultural land of West
Lancashire, Mere Sands
Wood is packed with interest
and activity.

Everyone, from young
children to keen naturalists,
will find something to please
on this reserve, which features
a mix of habitats including
varied woodland, dry heath,
grassland and lakes.

The reserve is an important habitat for water voles and supports lots of breeding woodland birds, dragonflies and over-wintering wildfowl.

Oak, rhododendron and beech were planted in the 19th century, but today's visitor will find birch, oak and a small, wartime plantation of Scots pine.

Once a thriving red squirrel population existed here but grey squirrels are now a more common sight. To entice the reds back, spruce and larch have been planted.

Access over this flat site is good, with well-surfaced paths and two waymarked trails. Paths suitable for wheelchair use were extended to 2km in the summer of 2003.

Ruff Wood
Ormskirk

Turn off A570 at Scarth Hill and then left into Ruff Lane. Ruff Wood approx. 200m on left. (SD426075)
8ha (20acres)

West Lancashire District Council

This wood is an isolated remnant, set within the sweeping landscape of the coastal plain.

Within the northern part is an old quarry with an exposed sandstone cliff that proves a popular feature, especially with younger visitors.

This outcrop of sandstone is a clue as to why this oak and birch woodland survives. Here the soils are thin and therefore of little value to agriculture. However, from the woodland edge you'll see a fertile plain coated in rich glacial deposits which made it ideal for growing crops.

The thin, acidic soil here is good for some plantlife including purple foxgloves, which appear late spring, brambles with their tasty blackberries in late summer, and bracken that turns from green to bronze in autumn.

This is an attractive woodland with a network of paths offering short routes.

MAP 3

Fairy Glen
Parbold

Turn off A5209 on to B5375. Turn down Stoneygate Lane. The entrance to Fairy Glen is at the far end of this lane. (SD517106)
10ha (24acres)
West Lancashire District Council

A path leading south through the valley begins with a gentle streamside walk and ends with a miniature gorge with waterfalls where Sprodley Brook cuts into the sandstone.

The brook meanders gently down a shallow gradient in a fairly broad valley to the north beneath a mixed broadleaved woodland of oak, rowan, alder, willow and beech on the drier valley sides. The giant hogweed grows here but shouldn't be touched as the sap can irritate your skin.

Ash and sycamore predominate in the south, with a spring covering of ramsons, bluebells and woodrush. This is a more dramatic landscape, with ferns, mosses and liverworts growing on exposed rock faces above the noisy brook.

Generally easy walking although steps may be slippery in the southern part of the wood.

Elnup Wood
Shevington, Nr Wigan

From B5206 turn down Park Brook Lane. Entrance to wood is on bend at end of road. (SD552090)
15ha (37acres)
Groundwork Wigan and Chorley

To find out how effectively woodland can transform industrial wasteland, you need look no further than Elnup Wood.

This ancient woodland was once the site of extensive coal mining operations yet the steep-sided valley of Mill Brook shows little evidence of this activity. Today it is managed as a community woodland, popular with local residents.

There are distinct areas within this predominantly broadleaved woodland, each with its own character. You'll find oak, birch, ash and hazel growing higher up the valley sides, mature beech trees on the steep slopes and some areas of younger regeneration. Below, the sound of Mill Brook can be heard as it flows gently over a series of small falls in the sandstone bedrock.

Mining relics, including coal tanks, can still be found within the wood but the mounds of excavated spoil along the valley floor have been colonised by sycamore.

Together with three adjoining woods, totalling over 34 hectares (84 acres), these form part of the Red Rose Forest.

Elnup Wood

MAP 3

Haigh Hall
Wigan / Aspull

Junction 27 on the M6, A49 to
Standish, followed by B5329 to
Haigh, or Junction 6 on the M6,
taking B5329 to Haigh. Haigh can
be found between A49 and A6.
(SD598085)
101ha (250acres)

Wigan MBC

A tapestry of broadleaved
woodland, the parkland around
Haigh Hall was first planted
more than 100 years ago. Today
it forms part of the Red Rose
Forest and provides an
important 'green corridor' into
the town of Wigan.

Here you can enjoy oak,
sycamore, birch, rowan, horse
chestnut and lime growing
alongside attractive areas of
beech with some lovely, majestic
specimens. The scenery changes
constantly, as beech glades
alternate with areas of dense
woodland and rhododendron –
enclosed spaces providing shade
and shelter.

More than 40 miles of paths
run through the site, including
three waymarked trails and a
good flat route allowing
wheelchairs and buggies to
access woodland nearest the hall
as well as other parts of the
grounds.

Lower down the hillside,
separated from the plantations
by Yellow Brook, is an ancient
woodland known as Bottling
Wood, which has a completely
different character since oak,
rather than beech, is the
dominant species.

Borsdane Wood
Hindley and Aspull

From Hindley head towards Westhoughton on A58, left into Hindley Mill Lane just before cemetry. Park in lane and walk ahead to unadopted road. Brick tunnel with barrier at front is pedestrian entrance. From Aspull take Bolton Road heading away from Wigan, turn into Mill Lane immediately after Gerrard Arms. Follow to cobbled road and park in open area then by foot over bridge and through metal squeeze stile. (SD624053)
27ha (67acres)
Wigan MBC

Families will love Borsdane Wood. Easy to find your way around, it offers parents peace and tranquility and provides youngsters with a safe and interesting place to explore.

Kind on eye and ear, particularly in spring and summer when alive with birdsong, this ancient woodland feels much larger than it is. The going is easy thanks to a dry, well-surfaced path that provides good buggy access. A series of smaller paths lead to footbridges crossing the stream.

You will find a tremendous variety of indigenous and planted species – among them oak, ash, birch, alder, horse chestnut, lime and wild cherry – not to mention sweet chestnut, sycamore, Turkey oak, poplars and willow. Occasional groups of beech provide a change of character while ground flora includes bluebell, wild garlic and butterbur.

This linear wood, which sits within the Red Rose Forest, has open farmland to either side with a number of pretty open glades in the southern end which would be perfect for picnics.

MAP 3

Lever Park

Horwich

Going north on A673 out of Horwich, turn right into Lever Park Avenue and 2km (1.5 miles) to Great House Barn car park. (SD635128)

152ha (376acres)

United Utilities

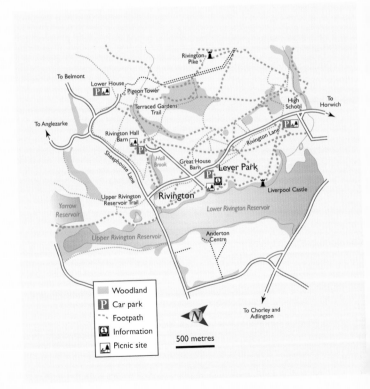

Lever Park

Beautiful woodland, fields and parkland draw thousands of people to Lever Park but, thanks to the abundance of tree cover, no visitor need ever feel part of a crowd.

The site – a large area of designed landscape – stands within what is now Rivington Country Park and stretches from the Rivington reservoirs and Horwich village over moorland up to Rivington Pike.

Industrial philanthropist Lord Leverhulme, who owned the estate at the turn of the 20th century, had a passion for landscaping which he was able to indulge fully here.

Tree-lined avenues and numerous woodland areas provide a delightful variety of trees from oak, birch and beech to sycamore, horse chestnut and sweet chestnut.

Lord Leverhulme called on the renowned landscape architect Thomas Mawson to help him create impressive hillside gardens around his residence beneath Rivington Pike.

After the war, much of the garden was allowed to become

83

MAP 3

Lever Park

overgrown but recent work by volunteers has reopened paths, allowing some of the most stunning features of the estate to re-emerge.

Today children in particular can enjoy a magical experience, exploring the 'secret' features that lie practically hidden among the woodlands beneath the Pigeon Tower on Rivington Moor, site of Lord Leverhulme's residence.

It is a place where the young can get swept up in make-believe, exploring the maze of terraces and steps and discovering the ponds, falls, follies and lawns that once adorned the windswept hillside.

And while the children indulge their imagination, grown-ups can discover the gardens in more detail. A trail leaflet available from the Great House information centre provides a plan and descriptions to help visitors explore the gardens and identify the remaining features.

Walker Fold Woodlands
Bolton

Turn off B6226 Chorley Old Road onto Walker Fold Road at Bob's Smithy Inn. Restricted parking is approx 1.6km (1 mile) on the left-hand side opposite cottages just before the wood. (SD676124) 18ha (44acres)

Bolton MBC

Nestling in a valley in open hill country, Walker Fold Woodland is a contrasting combination of conifer plantations and remnants of the oak woodland that must once have covered the Pennines.

Much of the site is coniferous – Japanese larch and Scots pine planted in the late 1950s – but cover is not dense, with numerous open areas. Well made, if occasionally muddy, footpaths link with the surrounding hills, creating potential for interesting short walks and lovely country views.

Attractive woodland covers several steep cloughs. Nearby are many areas of recently planted broadleaves – part of a programme which is helping to create the Red Rose Forest.

Wood sorrel growing in patches beneath the conifers contrasts with pink purslane that abounds in the deciduous woodland. Common valerian and common spotted orchid grow sporadically in the nearby field.

Roe deer live in the woodland while long-eared owls populate the surrounding hills and an upland stream running through the wood provides a habitat for grey wagtails.

MAP 3

High Shores Clough Woodland
Bolton

Exit the A58 Bolton ring road at Moss Bank Park traffic lights onto Barrow Bridge Road. The Barrow Bridge car park is approx 1.6km (1 mile) along this road on the left. (SD686118)
17ha (42acres)
Bolton MBC

High Shores is typical of the distinctive clough woodlands which lead down from the moors.

Compare this with nearby Raveden Wood (see page 88), another clough woodland which was replanted when it became incorporated into the landscape for Smithills Hall.

While ferns, Himalayan balsam and hogweed line the stream's edge, higher up the valley the ground cover is more typical of moorland and includes bilberry.

A short circular walk, full of variety, climbs up through the woodland and on to the moorland. From here lovely views extend across open countryside and it is a perfect spot for a picnic. The return route takes you down the 63 steps originally used by miners to reach the mines and quarries on the moors.

The scale of the woodland is ideal for children who will enjoy the small stream and counting the steps. A visit to the Smithills Hall visitor farm could complete a day out for both the young at heart and of mind.

Wilderswood
Horwich, Bolton

Turn off B6266 Chorley Old Road onto Georges Lane. Go straight on for approx 1.6km (1 mile) to car park at main gate to woodland. (SD652125)
9ha (22acres)
Bolton MBC

Planted on an exposed hillside during the second half of the last century, Wilderswood packs a lot of interest into a short walk.

The shelter of this plantation woodland, which is fairly dense in parts, contrasts effectively with surrounding open moorland and provides panoramic views over the surrounding countryside which includes the Red Rose Forest. From the western edge you can gaze across Horwich to the coast beyond.

A varied network of well-marked, sometimes muddy paths serves some interesting landmarks, including a disused quarry on the western boundary and the site of an old house. Young beech trees planted along Old Rake Way above the quarry create an attractive miniature avenue.

In the heart of the wood is the site of an old house, Rock Haven Castle. Though nothing of the house remains, you might discover the remnants of a walled garden, with cherries, damsons, raspberry canes and faint signs of the original paths.

Jumbles Country Park
Bolton

Take A676 signposted Ramsbottom. The A676 takes a sharp right turn at the Crofter's Arms into Bradshaw Road. Approx 1.6km (1 mile) on left is Jumbles Country Park and car park. (SD737139)
22ha (54acres)
United Utilities

The name Jumbles is a variation of 'dumbles', a northern term for a ravine with wooded sides down which tumbles a fast-flowing stream. The fast-flowing stream today is a serene reservoir, lying in the valley of Bradshaw Brook and surrounded by scenic trails through woods and meadows.

There's plenty to do here. You can watch birdlife from hides, fish or try out watersports in the reservoir (permits required), bring a picnic, visit the exhibition centre and take part in events.

A 4.5 km (3 mile) circular trail around the reservoir, which starts and finishes at the Waterfold car park, is suitable for wheelchair users. Look for wild orchids growing along the bank.

Where water from the reservoir is slowed down by large stones you may see a wagtail, dipper or kingfisher.

MAP 3

Raveden Wood, Smithills Hall Estate

Bolton

Turn off A58 Bolton Ring Road onto Smithills Dean Road. Approx 800m (0.5 mile) turn right into Smithills Hall and car parks. (Also signposted from A666 going north. Follow sign and then go straight across at traffic lights at Ring Road junction into Smithills Dean Road.) (SD700120)

19ha (47acres)

Bolton MBC

With its blend of ancient woodland, newer planting and formal landscaping, Raveden is a steep clough woodland which was added to the Smithills Hall estate in Victorian times. The rolling landscape with exposed rock faces and small streams provide interest and incident.

At the northern end, a thick canopy of trees and understorey of rhododendron enclose the path which runs alongside a meandering stream with a waterfall. Further down, the clough opens into an area dominated by beech where dappled sunlight reaches the woodland floor.

The scenery changes as you move further down and oak and sycamore replace beech

Raveden Wood

with a dense understorey of young saplings.

A main path loops through the woodland, leading to smaller paths and bridges that cross the stream. Children in particular will enjoy exploring this area.

Extend your visit to nearby High Shores Clough Woodland on the edge of the moors to see a wood of contrasting character within the Red Rose Forest.

Phillips Park
Whitefield, Manchester

Turn off A665 Higher Lane into Park Lane. Entrance to park is at end of lane. (SD796040)

13ha (32acres)

Bury MBC

A walk through mixed deciduous woodland on the hillside of Phillips Park is an ever-changing experience.

Along the top of the beech, sycamore, oak and pine-adorned slopes are attractive walks with open views across Manchester and the Red Rose Forest, of which this is a part. Large hollies are a feature of this area.

As you descend into the valley, patches of birch, rowan and oak give way to poplar, elm, lime and willow where hogweed, willowherb, butterbur and ramson grow along the damp riverside. At the base of the valley, the woodland becomes more enclosed and sheltered.

Emerge from the woods and you find yourself in patches of open grassland. Willowherb, meadowsweet and common spotted orchid grow in the valley meadows while, on higher ground, more orchids grow among clumps of willow.

A network of paths creates a number of circular walks. A pond, complete with viewing platform, is worth discovering in the wood.

MAP 3

Heaton Park
Prestwich, Manchester

Entrances signposted from Old
Bury Road (A665) and Sheepfoot
Lane (A6044). (SD830044)
259ha (640acres)

Manchester City Council

One of the largest parks in
Europe, it has an array of
attractions including
playgrounds and a farm, set on
a gently rolling landscape criss-
crossed with streams and
ponds. An extensive network of
paths leads through swathes of
woodland areas to contrasting
open grassland where Highland
cattle graze.

Scattered birch trees dot the
grassland, lending an attractive
parkland feel. In contrast, more
cultivated gardens are set
around the hall and farm.

Move into the woods and
there is another change of
mood with a varied blend of
oak, beech, sycamore and horse
chestnut which range from
open sections that invite
exploration, to wilder parts
with a dense understorey.

Blackley Forest
Blackley, Manchester

Turn off A576 into Blackley New
Road. Entrance to wood 250m on
left. Also entrance at north end of
site from Victoria Avenue off A576,
Middleton Road. (SD840034)
21ha (52acres)

Manchester City Council

Once inside, the sounds of
river and birdsong mask the
hum of nearby traffic, making
it possible to forget how close
you are to the centre of
Manchester.

Open glades on the hillside
provide views across to the
woods and grasslands of
Heaton Park – a surprisingly
rural prospect for such an
urban setting.

Managed as a community
woodland since 1953, this is a
real haven for people and
wildlife alike. There is a
network of paths including an
easily accessible walk alongside
the river.

Oak sapling

MAP 3

Tandle Hill Country Park
Royton

From A671 through Royton turn into Tandle Hill Road, following signs to Country Park. Car park at end of this road. (SD906086)
23ha (56acres)
Oldham MBC

If you are looking for a unique woodland experience, visit Tandle Hill Country Park.

A hillside site with striking views towards Manchester, the almost exclusively beech wood is something of a rarity in the North West.

The dense beech canopy arrests any growth on the woodland floor and the wood seems stripped down to basic structural elements. Varied shapes of dark beech trunks are set against a rusty orange layer of leaf litter on an undulating woodland floor with a bright green canopy above, creating an almost sculptural effect.

Known for its toadstools and mushrooms, Tandle Hill also has a fascinating history. The first trees were planted in 1820 to prevent radicals practising marching and drilling following the Peterloo Massacre in Manchester.

Today the experience is a peaceful one. A good network of paths aids access to other areas of Scots pine and larch and some oak regeneration. Picnic tables are provided and wooden sculptures dot the site.

Strinesdale Countryside Area
Oldham

Signposted from A62 Huddersfield Road. Turn into Culvert Street approx. 2.5km (1.5 miles) from Oldham town centre. (SD958065)
25ha (62acres)
United Utilities

This attractive site, set in open countryside, is full of variety. Its mosaic of habitats includes two lakes, numerous ponds, community woodland and meadows created following de-commissioning of two reservoirs in 1992.

It is interesting to see young woodland planting as part of a variety of different habitats and this makes a pleasant contrast to walking through established woodland. Children will enjoy the variations within the site and the wetland habitats.

Older woodland, of birch, sycamore, rowan and pine with rhododendron planted along the shores of the original reservoirs, form a fringe around the newer planting.

There is a variety of routes including a well-surfaced, level path suitable for wheelchairs and pushchairs around lower Strinesdale.

Daisy Nook Country Park
Ashton-under-Lyne, Oldham

From A627 Ashton Road turn down Newmarket Road and then into Stannybrook Road. Entrance to Country Park immediately on right. Another car park off A627 approx 1km (0.75 mile) north of Newmarket Road turning. (SD922006)
36ha (89acres)

Oldham MBC

River and meadow, lake and woodland can all be found at Daisy Nook Country Park, on the Ashton canal.

Paths lead through a variety of habitats including historic Boodle Wood by the River Medlock where the sound of running water and birdsong add to the wood's peaceful quality.

There are many discoveries to be made in the mixed woodland. Look for planted specimens which remind visitors of the site's former existence as an arboretum for nearby Riversvale Hall, now in ruins. Beech trees once lined the drive and these have now colonised the valley side. From here, views extend across the river and, on sunny days, light catching the tall trunks bring the wood to life.

Flora – typical of riverside woodland – includes hogweed, meadowsweet, ramson, rushes and the invasive Himalayan balsam. Giant-leaved Butterbur edges the river. The wood is particularly rich in autumn fungi including fly agaric and dead men's fingers.

MAP 3

Acornfield Local Nature Reserve
Kirkby
From M57 junction 4 take A580 towards St Helens and turn left into Coopers Lane at traffic lights. At roundabout turn right into Perimeter Road and then next left into Spinney Road. There is a small lay-by on right. (SJ437976) 13ha (31acres)
Knowsley Borough Council

Here is a small wood packed with interest to delight all ages, and worth taking the time to explore.

Acornfield Plantation was originally planted for game cover on the basin mire which once dominated the Kirby area. The open bog that remains within the woodland is a fascinating remnant of a lost landscape.

A network of grassy rides and narrow, winding paths rides lead through wetland areas with stands of flag iris, a central open area of sphagnum bog, a pond rich with dragonflies and damselflies, drainage ditches where water voles have been spotted, and rich areas of bracken, birch and mixed deciduous woodland.

There is an attractive structure to the woodland areas where large spreading specimens of oak, beech, sweet chestnut and Scots pine survive amidst areas of regeneration and stands of birch and wild cherry. Rhododendron forms much of the shrub layer.

Some 70 bird species have been recorded, including great spotted woodpeckers, jays and owls.

Croxteth Country Park
Liverpool
From M57 take A580 and follow brown tourist signs to Croxteth Hall and Country Park. (SJ410940) 121ha (300acres)
Liverpool City Council

Slip away from the crowds who flock to Croxteth Country Park and visit quiet woodland corners – you could almost forget you are in the city.

A patchwork of fields and woodland, the park is rich in bird species including jays, nuthatches, blackcap, chiffchaff and great spotted woodpecker.

A good network of paths provides plenty of opportunities to explore more remote corners of the park. Most of the woods feature typical estate planting and include ash, beech, sycamore, lime, sweet and horse chestnut, Scots and black pine and some impressive oaks including the unusual Lucombe variety.

There are replanted areas, rich in ground flora such as bluebells, wood anemones, ramsons, red campion and moschatel. One of the richest is Mull Wood, where access is restricted though there are regular guided walks and a permit system in operation. Closer to the Hall is Wilderness Wood, an amenity wood with an attractive walk and a range of ornamental and native species.

Stockton's Wood, Speke Hall
Liverpool

Follow brown tourist signs to Speke Hall. (SJ420825)
57ha (141acres) SSSI
The National Trust

Size isn't everything, as Stockton's Wood proves. This lovely site has an ancient woodland feel despite its age, size and the presence of a neighbouring airport.

Dead and dying timber provides a valuable habitat for rare beetles while in spring the woodland floor has a vivid bluebell carpet.

Planted in the 17th century with oak, beech and sweet chestnut to provide timber for the Speke Hall estate, there is a sense of peace in the woodland interior.

Mature spreading trees grow among young birch with bramble and rhododendron beneath – the latter is earmarked for removal to help restore the wood's biodiversity. Dense undergrowth encircles more open areas and you can enjoy good views standing beneath the canopy of some lovely mature trees, including gnarled sweet chestnut and some unusual oaks apparently growing on 'stilts'.

Access is via a waymarked trail and some well-surfaced, level paths with wheelchair and buggy access in the southern section.

MAP 3

Upton Meadow Millennium Wood
Wirral, Merseyside

Lies on the northwestern tip of the Wirral peninsula close to the town of Birkenhead, between the villages of Upton and Greasby. (SJ265877)
1 1ha (27acres)
The Woodland Trust

Nestling in an intensely urban area close to Birkenhead, Upton Meadow is an oasis for people and wildlife alike.

It encompasses a network of ecologically important habitats. But it is also a vital recreational resource for local people, who make good use of some 1.5 km of footpaths. The public bridleway along its western boundary provides an important link for the people of Upton and Greasby to Arrowe Park and beyond.

Well-loved and used, the woodland, a wide and varied mix of native broadleaves and shrubs, was created as part of the Woodland Trust's 'Woodlands on Your Doorstep' initiative.

Visitors can explore the lowland tree mix of Upton Bridge Wood or enjoy the grassland on Southern Meadow. A pond in the north of the site sustains many invertebrates and amphibians – including a healthy toad population.

Arrowe Brook, which marks the west boundary, is an excellent wildlife corridor with a rich mix of plants, shrubs and trees along its bank.

Storeton Wood
Higher Bebington

Close to Storeton and Higher Bebington, entrances via Marsh Lane, Mount Road and Resthill Road. (SJ313849)
1 3ha (3 1 acres)
The Woodland Trust

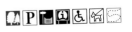

Today Storeton is a tranquil oasis in an urban landscape – complete with butterflies, birds and even dinosaur footprints!

The fossilised prints are believed to belong to a raptor-like dinosaur which was named after the location, *Cheirotherium storeonia*. Centuries old, they only came to light in the 1920s and are now housed in

Dinosaur carving in Storeton Wood

Liverpool Museum and the British Museum.

On the site of an old sandstone quarry dating back to Roman times, the woods may be dismissed by some as merely a patch of secondary woodland on an urban fringe. However, Storeton is located in one of the least wooded parts of the UK and enjoyed all the more by local residents.

Careful and enthusiastic management has created a wildlife haven where butterflies such as the red admiral and small copper and birds including jay, lesser spotted woodpecker and kestrels thrive. The Trust receives considerable support from the Friends of Storeton Woods who helped to purchase the wood and still today raise funds and organise workdays to help conserve this valuable woodland.

MAP 3

Stanney Wood
Little Stanney
A5117 from M53, west of Little
Stanney. Signposted from A5117.
(SJ397738)
9ha (22acres)
Ellesmere Port & Neston BC

This remnant of ancient wet
woodland was originally part
of one of the four Crown
Forests of Cheshire.

Tucked between road and
housing, this parcel of land
boasts a surprisingly attractive
variety of trees including oak,
sycamore, birch, hazel, elder and
holly. Beneath the tall mature
specimens there is a healthy
younger generation emerging.

A choice of three
waymarked routes, including a
'healthy trail', pass through the
wood on level, well-surfaced
paths. These are popular with
local people who enjoy the
pleasant short strolls. A further
network of minor paths invites
exploration of the quieter parts
of the wood.

The site was recognised for
its importance to local wildlife
by being designated a Local
Nature Reserve in 1993.

Little Budworth Country Park
Little Budworth

At junction of A49/A54 follow sign for Little Budworth, main car park on left in southeast corner of site. (SJ587657)

33ha (82acres) SSSI

Cheshire County Council

Five miles from Delamere Forest lies Little Budworth Country Park Woods, a woodland remnant of the evocatively named ancient hunting forest of Mara and Mondrum.

Much of the sandy heathland site is covered with birch woodland plus oak, holly and beech. Sunny open clearings and small areas of open water add to the interest of this varied site.

The flowers – mainly gorse and heather – are typical of heathland, as are many of the wildlife species, including woodcock and green hairstreak butterfly.

Exploration of this attractive site makes for some easy walking, thanks to the level paths. There are no very large trees to dominate the scene and the woodland floor is generally open with scattered ferns allowing views across the woods.

Although the woods are dense in places, with light filtering through the birch-dominated canopy to cast a dappled shade on the woodland floor, it never feels oppressive.

MAP 3

Delamere Forest
Northwich & Chester

Turn north off A556 on to B5152, turn left just before Delamere Station, follow road to visitor centre. (SJ547705)

430ha (1063acres) SSSI

Forestry Commission

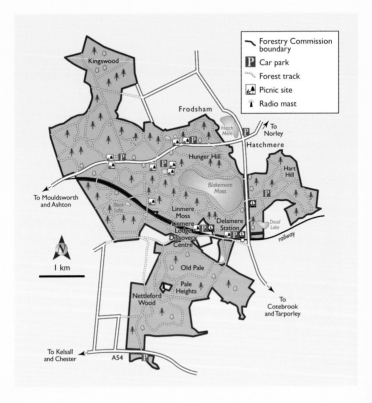

Cheshire's largest area of woodland, Delamere Forest is a remnant of the ancient forest of Mara and Mondrum and offers some wonderful walks to delight and interest the visitor.

The forest has an interesting background. Once rich in game – red and roe deer and wild boar – it became the exclusive hunting ground of the Earls of Chester and protected by Forest Law.

Later the site was exploited for peat, sand and gravel and eventually much of it reverted to heathland. After World War I it was planted with conifers and today is dominated by Corsican pine, though there are some large broadleaved areas with oak and sweet chestnuts.

Today this great mix of habitats, including mosses and meres, supports a colourful mix of birds including great spotted and green woodpeckers, siskins and crossbills. Delamere is well known for its dragonfly and damselfly populations – no fewer than 15 different species have been recorded.

Thanks to an extensive network of forest rides and paths throughout the site, there is ample opportunity to explore the myriad of habitats tucked among the trees.

Delamere Forest

MAP 3

Delamere Forest

Blakemere Moss is a developing 'schwingmoor' – a carpet of sphagnum moss floating over fluid peat and water. Here you might spot unusual plants such as the carnivorous sundew.

Another lake on the site – Hatch Mere – is worth seeking out as it offers plenty of opportunity for birdwatching.

A recent development at Delamere is a wetland experiment. The work is focussed on a former mire that was originally drained by Napoleonic prisoners who were drafted in to work after the Battle of Waterloo.

Foresters are felling trees and building sluices across drains as part of a project aimed at restoring the site to its natural state.

Helsby Hill
Helsby

Exit 14 off M56, follow A56
toward Helsby. Take right fork
(Robin Hood Lane) for 1km
(0.75 mile) then left at crossroads.
Car park 800m (0.5 mile) on left.
(SJ492745)
15ha (37acres)
The National Trust

Overlooking the Mersey stands
the lovely small woodland of
Helsby Hill where rocky
sandstone outcrops add drama
to the scenery.

Easy walking with short,
not-too-difficult climbs takes
the visitor up through the
woodland of oak, birch, holly
and rowan and a ground cover
of ferns and bracken, to the
summit of Helsby Hill.

Towards the top of the hill
the trees have become shaped
and stunted by the wind and
the wood eventually gives way
to bare rock and pockets of
heath vegetation.

One path winds up past
craggy outcrops and trees
and out between tall
hedgerows to a field before
joining another path that
leads back into the wood and
out onto the summit – a lovely
short walk full of incident
and drama.

From here the visitor can
take in splendid panoramic
views north across the Mersey,
west into Wales and to the
south and east across the
Cheshire countryside.

Helsby Hill

MAP 3

Woodhouse Hill, Snidley Moor & Frodsham Hill Woods
Frodsham

Located 1.6km (1 mile) southwest of Frodsham, adjoining Snidley Moor Wood (SJ513752) in southeast corner. Frodsham Hill Wood (SJ519771) is on the southwest outskirts of Frodsham/Overton and 1km (0.75 mile) northeast of Woodhouse Hill Wood. (SJ510754) 54ha (133acres)

The Woodland Trust

Sited on a prominent sandstone escarpment in northwest Cheshire, these undulating woods offer far-reaching views from the Welsh borders to the western Pennines and the Bowland Fells.

There is a rich history to be discovered here. At the summit of Woodhouse Hill the remains of an Iron Age fort can be made out, now designated a Scheduled Ancient Monument, and Snidley Moor's surviving patches of heather and bilberry suggest a long history of being grazed heath with woodland.

Over 3km of footpaths, including a section of the Sandstone Trail, cross and link the sites which form the second largest continuous block of broadleaved woodland in Cheshire.

Big Wood
Runcorn

On the northeastern edge of Runcorn adjacent to Norton Priory. (SJ551830) 9ha (23acres)

The Woodland Trust

Big Wood, on the edge of the historic Norton Priory site, has a chequered history.

Once part of the Norton manor estate, it passed to the Brookes family following the dissolution. They created woodland walks and pleasure gardens, transforming the site in the mid 18th century.

Dramatic changes continued until 1874 when new paths and vistas were created. However, after the Brookes family left the house in 1921, Big Wood's fortunes suffered. The Runcorn Expressway halved the site and more

Big Wood

pressure came from housing development.

Things began to improve in the 1980s when major improvements were made to the footpaths and since then a pond, ditch and woodland restoration programme, including the removal of more than 2 hectares of invasive rhododendron, has been completed.

Today the woodland boasts a good mix of trees and shrubs, including pendunculate and turkey oak, sycamore, alder, silver birch and yew, with a large pond at its heart.

MAP 3

Owley Wood
Weaverham

A49 to Weaverham then B5142
and B5153. Past shopping area,
turn left into Wallerscote Road
and left into Owley Wood Road.
(SJ625743)
6ha (15acres)

Cheshire Wildlife Trust

Peace, broken only by the
sound of birdsong and the
gentle movement of the River
Weaver, is one of the prime
delights of Owley Wood.

This ancient clough
woodland clothes the steep
east-facing slope of the
river valley.

Managed as a community
woodland for almost a decade
and home to a variety of
woodland birds, this is a
broadleaved wood of sycamore,
ash and alder with a rich
understorey of hazel, hawthorn,
holly, elder and goat willow.

Adding to the character of
the wood are some lovely
mature oak and sweet chestnut
trees. Small streams flowing
down the slope feed into a
river where ducks and swans
can often be seen swimming.

Well-surfaced paths and
boardwalk sections provide a
circular walk along the
riverside and up the slope to
the top of the wood for a
lovely view overlooking the
river and valley.

Marbury Country Park
Comberbach / Northwich

1.6km (1 mile) north of
Northwich, entrance off
Comberbach/Barnton road. From
A559 follow brown tourist signs to
country park. (SJ654762)
86ha (213acres)

Cheshire County Council

If you are looking for a walk
full of interest and variety,
make a visit to Marbury
Country Park.

Marbury Hall is long gone
but the parkland of the old
estate remains and the
woodlands that fringe the park
provide gentle but feature-
filled walks along well-surfaced
paths through woods of
contrasting character.

Big Wood, which lies along
the southern shore of
Budworth Mere, has occasional
clearings amongst oak, ash,
sycamore and chestnut plus
small ponds and a hide to
watch woodland birds such as
chiffchaff and willow warbler.
Bluebells and wood anemones
provide a fine spring show.

Further along, the wood
runs parallel with the Cheshire
Ring Canal and the mood
changes with birch and Scots
pine taking centre stage. The
path continues into Hopyard
Wood, a broadleaved area
within the valley of the gently
meandering Cogshall Brook.
Here the understorey is denser
and the wood darker and
more enclosed.

Bluebells adding their spring colour

Park Moss

Park Moss
Arley, Warrington

From Appleton take Arley Road south. Cross over the M56 and follow road for about 3km (2 miles). Woodland entrance on left. (SJ660817)

10ha (24acres)

The Woodland Trust

Park Moss Wood is located to the south of Warrington and near the village of Arley.

When acquired by the Woodland Trust in 1985 a section of Corsican pine was cleared to make way for a mix of broadleaves including oak, cherry, rowan, hazel and alder to be planted. Visit this section to see a wood in the making.

The slim white trunks of silver birch predominate with oak, Scots pine, willow, holly, alder, wild cherry and alder buckthorn among the other trees to be found here. Distinctive fronds of different varieties of fern texture the woodland floor in a variety of lush greens.

As the wood's name implies, the site lies on a peaty, low-lying remnant of mossland. A series of open ditches surround the wood to aid drainage.

Access is good – the site contains two public rights of way – although visitors in winter are advised that the ground can become very wet indeed.

Lumb Brook Valley
Warrington

Lies in the Appleton area of south Warrington. Park on Dingle Lane. (SJ627849)

9ha (22acress)

The Woodland Trust

You get four woods for the 'price' of one as Lumb Brook Valley is in reality a collection of interconnected but distinctive woodland sites.

The Fords Rough contains an area of ancient woodland while, in the valley, you will discover a diverse range of shrubs and flowers. A surfaced, if sometimes waterlogged, footpath provides access through the length of the wood.

The Dingle is a large wooded valley offering a variety of broadleaf and conifers. A well-used footpath meanders through sparse ground vegetation but pockets of colourful flowers emerge here each spring. Under pressure from development, the site was extended by the Woodland Trust in 1998 to buffer the woodland from the impact of farming on one side and housing on the other.

By contrast, Long Wood has many maturing oaks with dense layers of rhododendron beneath.

Add nearby 17-acre Grappenhall Heys (SJ630856) and 20-acre Grappenhall Wood (SJ641858) to your visit and you could explore six woods in one day.

Lumb Brook Valley

MAP 3

Risley Moss
Warrington

M62, Junction 11, follow A574 over three roundabouts following signs to Risley Moss. (SJ663921)
10ha (25acres) SSSI
Warrington Borough Council

In this rare surviving fragment of the boggy wasteland that once dotted the Mersey Valley lie the woodlands of Risley Moss.

You will discover a pleasant mosaic of dense birch and sunny clearings – many sculptures too – with seats and benches located at regular intervals along well-surfaced woodland paths.

Peat was harvested from the Moss in the 1800s and, during World War II, a munitions factory occupied part of the site. After the war it became derelict and wildlife reclaimed once again. Its abundant pond life and dragonflies earned the site SSSI and Local Nature Reserve status.

A hide and an observation tower provide vantage points to view barn owls, hobbies, hen harriers and other wildlife. While public access to the Moss itself is restricted to guided walks, you can gain a closer view of this important wildlife habitat by studying the series of small ponds found in the woodland.

Also worth a visit nearby is the Woodland Trust's 17-hectare Gorse Covert Mounds (SJ665928).

Styal Estate
Styal

From A57 take Manchester Airport exit. Follow signs to Quarry Bank Mill. Signs from Wilmslow. (SJ836829)
50ha (124 acres)
The National Trust

Adorning a deep valley, carved by the River Bollin through sandstone bedrock, the meandering broadleaved woodland of the Styal Estate is a haven for a variety of wildlife.

Fungi adorn the ancient trees in which woodpeckers thrive, while bluebells carpet the woodland floor in spring.

The estate incorporates Quarry Bank Mill, an apprentice house, mill workers' village and 300 acres of countryside in the Bollin Valley, all managed by the National Trust.

Mainly broadleaves, complemented by planted beech, hornbeam, Scots pine and exotics such as Wellingtonia, the woods have many impressive mature specimens and are full of interest, with plenty to please the visitor.

Walking through the southern section is easy on dry, level and sandy paths. From the mill to Tweenies bridge is suitable for wheelchairs and buggies. The going gets harder in the steeper northern woods where boots are a must.

Alderley Edge
Alderley Edge

From Alderley Edge village take B5087 Macclesfield Road. Car park 1.6km (1 mile) on left after Wizard Inn. (SJ860775)
120ha (297acres) SSSI

The National Trust

Magical Alderley Edge is the stuff of myth and legend – no wonder people love it.

There is a special atmosphere on this site with its medieval earthworks, England's oldest copper mines, beacon and legend-shrouded Wizard's Well that draws the crowds, especially at weekends.

Visit during the week or in the early morning and evening if you want to freely explore. The site's rich history and legends form an important part of local folklore and inspired Alan Garner's popular book *The Weirdstone of Brisingamen*.

It is a delightful place to walk with so much to discover that it is possible to return many times and still find something new. Children love the woods with its sandstone cliffs, caves and mine entrances, or hunting for the Well.

An extensive network of paths leads to Stormy Point – where visitors throng to enjoy wonderful views of the surrounding countryside.

MAP 3

Macclesfield Forest

Macclesfield Forest
Macclesfield

A523 south from Macclesfield, turn left toward Langley, through village then right beside reservoir and first left up towards the ranger centre and main car park.
(SJ961714)
400ha (989acres)
United Utilities

There is magic in Macclesfield Forest, a large conifer-dominated woodland set around three reservoirs on the slopes of the Peak District hills overlooking the Cheshire Plain.

The most extensive area of broadleaf trees can be found in Brick Kiln Wood, high on the hill above the Trentabank reservoir, where beautiful mature sycamores cling to the side of the hill.

Visitors are well cared for in the forest, with the felling of conifers making way for native broadleaves and the creation of an excellent network of well-surfaced paths.

As a result, there is a choice of routes, from low-level ambles near the reservoirs with their resident wildfowl to more challenging walks through dense conifer plantations out onto the open moorland above and a wonderful vantage point from the summit of Sutlingsloe, Cheshire's second highest point.

Many woodland birds thrive in the plantation and one stand of tall trees supports Cheshire's largest heronry – a handy viewpoint is provided nearby.

Brereton Heath Country Park

Holmes Chapel / Congleton

A54 from Holmes Chapel. After 2.5km (1.5 miles) turn right into Davenport Lane, entrance 450m on left. Site is signposted. (SJ800650)
34ha (84acres)

Cheshire County Council

A mosaic of birch, oak, Scots pine and holly fringes the large lake in this country park which lies within the flat rural landscape of the Cheshire Plain.

The woodlands are peaceful and provide an interesting short walk on level ground. The Brimstone Trail leads past a series of sculptures, created on site by a variety of artists over recent years, and features such highlights as the *Oak Drum* and *Wings in the Wood*. A wheelchair-accessible route follows the perimeter of the lake.

The wealth of bird life includes great and lesser spotted woodpeckers, nuthatch, treecreepers and goldfinch in the woodland, kingfisher, heron and great crested grebe around the lake.

A variety of activities can be explored here from cycling, orienteering, angling and canoeing to picnics and willow basket making. Dogs do not have to be on leads as long as they are under control.

MAP 3

Bickerton Hills
Bickerton

A534 to Bickerton then right at
church. After 1km (0.75 mile) turn
right into Pool Lane Car Park.
(SJ505530)
28ha (69acres) SSSI
The National Trust

On a sandstone ridge rising
out of the Cheshire plain are
the hills of Bickerton, Bulkeley
and Peckforton – three
broadleaved woodlands
offering a great day out.

Bickerton Hill woods are
mainly birch with oak, rowan
and holly, encircling open
heath vegetation of gorse,
bracken and heather on
the summit.

A gentle climb leads to the
summit. An Iron Age hillfort –
Maiden Castle – stands on the
wild but peaceful ridge which
boasts panoramic views – a
gentle contrast with the distant
hum of life on the Cheshire
Plain. The remains of earth
banks that protected the huts
inside are still visible. From
here buzzards may be seen
circling, their distinctive
mewing call a familiar sound at
certain times of the year.

Other wildlife to look out
for includes the green
hairstreak butterfly which feeds
on bilberries during the
summer. The woodland
supports many birds and flocks
of tits are common in autumn
and winter.

A walk through the nearby
oak woods of Bulkeley Hill,
also owned by the National

Trust, is equally inspiring. The path leads to a summit scattered with huge sweet chestnuts where views extend to the Peak District, Cannock Chase and the Wrekin. To reach the wood turn off the A534 at Bulkeley toward Peckforton, access at the junction of Stonehouse Lane and Mill Lane.

Public access to the estate woodland of Peckforton Hills may not be as free but there is a good network of paths. Before entering the woodland, via the entrance to Peckforton Castle, take special note of the Wesley oak opposite – one of the oldest trees in Cheshire and named after John Wesley who was said to have preached beneath it in 1749. Keep your eye out for birdlife which includes pied flycatcher and crossbill.

Tower Hill
Malpas

Turn west at Cholmondeley Arms crossroads on A49, entrance to Cholmondeley Castle 200m on right. Woodland within grounds of castle. (SJ549506)
8ha (20acres)
The Marquess of Cholmondeley

Set on a low hill on the edge of Cholmondeley Castle, views can be enjoyed over the castle's gardens to one side and the rolling Cheshire countryside to the other. The wooded Bickerton Hills (see previous entry) and Peckforton ridge are a feature of the vista.

The woods are reached by walking through the castle gardens which contain some stately trees including a lovely spreading oak which the path passes.

Beneath beech, oak, lime, sweet chestnut and Scots pine you will discover patches of rhododendron which erupt into colour each spring. By contrast, the interior is planted with beech. The mix is good for birds with older trees providing a good food source for woodpeckers.

This is a short, easy walk on grassy paths which can get muddy after rain.

WOODLAND
TRUST

Trees and forests are crucial to life on our planet. They generate oxygen, play host to a spectacular variety of wildlife and provide us with raw materials and shelter. They offer us tranquillity, inspire us and refresh our souls.

Founded in 1972, the Woodland Trust is now the UK's leading woodland conservation charity. By acquiring sites and campaigning for woodland it aims to conserve, restore and re-establish native woodland to its former glory. The Trust now owns and cares for over 1,100 woods throughout the UK.

The Woodland Trust wants to see:
no further loss of ancient woodland
the variety of woodland wildlife restored and improved
an increase in new native woodland
an increase in people's understanding and enjoyment of woodland

The Woodland Trust has in excess of 170,000 members who share this vision. For every new member, the Trust can care for approximately half an acre of native woodland. For details of how to join the Woodland Trust please either ring FREEPHONE 0800 026 9650 or visit the website at www.woodland-trust.org.uk.

If you have enjoyed the woods in this book please consider leaving a legacy to the Woodland Trust. Legacies of all sizes play an invaluable role in helping the Trust to create new woodland and secure precious ancient woodland threatened by development and destruction. For further information please either call 01476 581129 or visit our dedicated website at www.legacies.org.uk

Lumb Brook Valley

Further Information

Public transport

Each entry gives a brief description of location, nearest town and grid reference. Traveline provides impartial journey planning information about all public transport services either by ringing 0870 608 2608 (calls charged at national rates) or visit www.traveline.org.uk. For information about the Sustrans National Cycle Network either ring 0117 929 0888 or visit www.sustrans.org.uk

Useful contacts

Forestry Commission, 0845 367 3787, www.forestry.gov.uk
National Trust, 0870 458 4000, www.nationaltrust.org.uk
Wildlife Trusts, 0870 036 7711, www.wildlifetrusts.org
RSPB, 01767 680551, www.rspb.org.uk
Royal Forestry Society, 01442 822028, www.rfs.org.uk
Tree Council, 020 7407 9992, www.treecouncil.org.uk
National Forest, 01283 551211, www.nationalforest.org
Woodland Trust, 01476 581111, www.woodland-trust.org.uk

Recommend a Wood

You can play a part in helping us complete this series. We are inviting readers to nominate a wood or woods they think should be included. We are interested in any woodland with public access in the UK.

To recommend a wood please photocopy this page and provide as much of the following information as possible:

About the wood

Name of wood: _____

Nearest town: _____

Approximate size: _____ ha/acres

Owner/manager: _____

A few words on why you think it should be included:

_____

_____

About you

Your name: _____

Your postal address: _____

_____

_____ Post code: _____

If you are a member of the Woodland Trust please provide your membership number.

Please send to: Exploring Woodland Guides, The Woodland Trust, Autumn Park, Dysart Road, Grantham, Lincolnshire NG31 6LL, by fax on 01476 590808 or e-mail woodlandguides@woodland-trust.org.uk

Thank you for your help

Other Guides in the Series

Chilterns to the
Welsh Borders

The South West
of England

The South East
of England

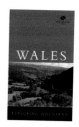

Wales

The Peak District
& Central England

East Anglia &
North Thames

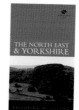

The North East
& Yorkshire

Coming soon
Scotland

If you would like to be notified when certain titles are due for publication please either write to Exploring Woodland Guides, The Woodland Trust, Autumn Park, Dysart Road, Grantham, Lincolnshire NG31 6LL or e-mail woodlandguides@woodland-trust.org.uk

Index